Holy Faith of Santa Fe

1863-2000

Holy Faith of Santa Fe
1863-2000

Stanford Lehmberg

LPD Press, Albuquerque

For information: LPD Press
925 Salamanca NW
Albuquerque, NM 87107-5647
Telephone: (505) 344-9382
www.nmsantos.com

Book and cover design by Paul Rhetts & Barbe Awalt

Library of Congress Control Number 2003112871

ISBN 1-890689-12-2

First Edition
10 9 8 7 6 5 4 3 2 1

Contents

Illustrations

Color Photographs
by Derek Lehmberg

Foreword

Several years ago, the Church of the Holy Faith was privileged to accept a long-time Episcopalian and historian of distinction, Dr. Stanford Lehmberg, as a transferred member from Minnesota. Dr. Lehmberg is one of the finest historians of the Reformation in England, and a scholar of Anglicanism from the Reformation and before, through the nineteenth century. After he provided several summers of well-received lectures on various aspects of Anglican history, the vestry inquired about his writing a history of the Church of the Holy Faith and its fascinating role in the political and cultural life of Santa Fe since the mid-1860s.

The Church of the Holy Faith has witnessed to the Gospel of Our Lord for over one hundred and thirty years. In that time it has experienced ups and downs with a number of remarkable lay and clergy leaders, most of them included in this book. It is a very colorful history which will help fill in some important gaps in Santa Fe's past, and so lively that the vestry provided Dr. Lehmberg with complete editorial control, knowing that otherwise, several "lay popes" with family lineages here might attempt to "airbrush" some of the past involving their renowned forebears. (This is not unknown in Christian church histories!)

It is a pleasure to commend this history of a wonderful parish church to what I hope will be a wide readership. Dr. Lehmberg has provided a rich narrative along with a superb selection of pictures and photographs to accompany his text. We are grateful for the honor he has done this church, and we hope this book contributes in some small way to the greater knowledge of the Southwest; to Santa Fe; and of course to this particular portion of the Body of Christ, in its two-thousand year life.

The Very Reverend Canon Dale D. Coleman
Rector, Church of the Holy Faith

Preface

The history of any church can engage the attention of its own members. The Church of the Holy Faith in Santa Fe, however, can claim the interest of a larger group of readers for several reasons. It is the oldest Episcopal church, and one of the oldest of any Protestant denomination, in New Mexico. Its early leaders, men like Governor L. Bradford Prince, Senator Thomas B. Catron, and Senator Bronson M. Cutting, were prominent in government and politics; their careers linked church and state in early twentieth-century Santa Fe. Some of its buildings were designed by the greatest architect of the Santa Fe style, John Gaw Meem, who, together with his wife Faith, was a loyal parishioner for many decades. Art work in the church includes a reredos by the well-known artist Gustave Baumann. The church's pipe organ is the largest in northern New Mexico and the music program has long-standing connections with the Santa Fe Opera. The earlier chapters of the Holy Faith history are thus part of the political and artistic history of Santa Fe and indeed New Mexico and the Southwest.

The life of the parish during the second half of the twentieth century is of interest for different reasons. Holy Faith provides a fascinating case study of problems affecting the Episcopal church throughout the United States during these years. It was subject to more serious divisions of opinion than most parishes and was heavily influenced by conservatives who deplored such actions as the ordination of women and homosexuals, the blessing of same-sex unions, Prayer Book revision, and the adoption of inclusive language. It disapproved of social action policies of the national church and withdrew its financial support from the national body. But it was exceptionally generous in its outreach and made significant grants to charitable organizations in the Santa Fe community, the United

States, and throughout the world. After a period of controversy and loss of members it ended the century at a new high point and seemed poised to continue its growth and service. Throughout its history the parish was led by a number of prominent churchmen, the most important of whom, C. J. Kinsolving, went on to become the bishop of New Mexico and Southwest Texas. Two more topics of continuing interest are the role of women in the life of the parish—in 2000 the Women's Guild held its 117th annual St. Nicholas Bazaar to raise money for charitable causes—and the importance of the parish library, one of the finest in the country.

In a way my own earlier work in studying the church in England prepared me to examine the history of Holy Faith. I had written about Henry VIII and the role of Parliament in the English Reformation, and I had published books about English cathedrals in the sixteenth and seventeenth centuries. The differences between a modern parish and a historic cathedral are perhaps not so great as one might think. In each case one faces ideological issues, personalities, and controversies, as well as the history of buildings, architecture, and music. The historian's job is to search the archives for the relevant information and then put it together, like pieces of a jig-saw puzzle, so that it forms a comprehensible pattern. Fortunately for this study, the archives of the Church of the Holy Faith proved to be unusually full, although they required sorting and arranging. Dealing with recent times raises special problems—one must attempt to be unbiased and try not to write anything that might be unfair or offensive to persons still living, an issue that does not face the historian of the sixteenth century. On the other hand it is possible to interview those who took part in important developments themselves and can illuminate matters that remain dark in the written records. I hope that the combination of traditional sources and personal insights comes through in part of what follows. Throughout I have attempted to be accurate, fair, and judicious. Any errors of fact or judgment are of course my own.

A list of acknowledgments must begin with thanking the present rector, the Rev. Dale Coleman, for asking me to undertake this project. I especially appreciated his insistence that the final form of the text should be mine, not his. I also benefitted from the comments of many people who read all or part of the manuscript. In addition to Fr. Coleman these include Kathryn Campbell, the Rev. Robert Dinegar, Professor Richard Frost, the Rev. Joan Garcia, Darlene and David Haskin, the Rev. Beth Noland, Mary Lou and Robert Mayhew, Dr. Noel Ice, the Rev. Phyllis Orbaugh, Richard and Jetta Simpson, Richard and Mary Lou Stark, Stephen Watkins, and Nancy Meem Wirth.

I am grateful to the Photo Archives in the Palace of the Governors in Santa Fe, the Center for Southwest Research in the Zimmerman Library at the University of New Mexico, and the Episcopal Church's Institute of Historical Survey in Mesilla Park, New Mexico, for permission to reproduce photographs from their collections. Joan Garcia and Noel Ice helped with copying photographs kept at the church. Photographs of the present clergy were taken by Harry Orbaugh. The colored pictures of the Holy Faith buildings and art works are taken from photographs made by my son, Derek Lehmberg. Dr. Evan Davies, the diocesan archivist, and his associates at the Institute answered several questions about statistics. Finally, I express thanks to my publishers, Barbe Awalt and Paul Rhetts, for their knowledgeable cooperation and enthusiasm for this project.

(1) Rt. Rev. Josiah Cruickshank Talbot, photographed at Triennial Convention of the Episcopal Church in 1862, from Beatrice Chauvenet, Holy Faith in Santa Fe.

1. "May the Lord Prosper Our Efforts," 1863-1882

The first parish register of the Church of the Holy Faith begins with an account of the earliest Episcopal services that were held in Santa Fe.

> The first official visitation of any Protestant Episcopal minister (of which there is any record) was that of Rt. Rev. Jos. Cruickshank Talbot, then Missionary Bishop of the Northwest, when he acted as chaplain to a civic & military 4th of July procession. July 5th next day (Sunday) he preached in the Presbyterian church after Morning Prayer by Rev. Wm. A. Rich and Rev. A. H. De Mora. After Evening Prayer by same, Rev. W. A. Rich preached. Bp. Talbot administered the communion according to the Reformed Ritual for the first time in New Mexico to 5 persons besides the clergy. July 12th (next Sunday), Morning Prayer in Spanish, Bp. Talbot preached. Evening prayer by same clergymen, Bp. Talbot preached, afternoon same Sunday Rev. A. H. De Mora preached in Spanish.[1]

This was in 1863.

Bishop Talbot had come by stage coach from Colorado. His diary records a dreadful trip, with drunken passengers singing obscene songs. Santa Fe was not much better; he found it "exceedingly unprepossessing . . . The streets are very narrow, uneven and dirty," and the people were guilty of "loose morals," "univer-

---

[1] Parish Register 1, p. 6. The early parish registers were kept in volumes devised by the Rev. Charles Wells Hayes, originally published in New York by the Church Book Society, subsequently by E. P. Dutton. They have sections for History, Families, Baptisms, Confirmations, Communicants, Marriages, Burials, Offerings, and Parochial Statistics.

sal concubinage," and "open adultery." At the request of a committee of local gentlemen Talbot had joined the Fourth of July procession and officiated as Chaplain of the day. His congregations on July 5 were large. The celebration of Holy Communion was "a truly interesting and deeply solemn occasion. Besides the clergymen, there were five who partook–among them the acting governor, Mr. Arny. The object in celebrating in the evening was to accommodate a communicant who was to leave the next morning and would probably have no other opportunity for years to come, and who, though confirmed eight years before, had never had an opportunity to partake till now." The following Sunday evening the Bishop baptized Mrs. Emma Cutler and confirmed her and Mr. George T. Beall. "These persons are valuable accession to the Church," he wrote. "May the Lord prosper our efforts to establish it!"[2]

During his visit Talbot met the Catholic bishop, Jean Baptiste Lamy, in the office of Captain McFerran at Fort Lamy and noted that they had a pleasant conversation about the territory. The Catholic church had of course been involved in New Mexico since the early days of Spanish colonization. Franciscans had accompanied Oñate to Quivira in 1601. The Franciscans returned after the Pueblo Revolt of 1680, but the church was neglected by the Mexican bishops of Durango, in whose diocese it lay. Lamy had come to Santa Fe from France in 1851 and was named bishop the following year. In 1869 he had begun construction of the present Catholic cathedral, built in the Romanesque style of his native Auvergne; he was responsible for establishing the College of St. Michael and the Loretto Academy. Several Protestant groups had also found their way to Santa Fe before Bishop Talbot's visit. A Baptist minister, Henry W. Reed, held services in 1849 and erected a modest adobe church which was consecrated in 1854. The Methodists sent the Rev. E. G. Nicholson to Santa Fe in 1850, but he conducted services for only two years before leaving the territory. In 1851 the first Presbyterian missionary, W. T. Kephardt, arrived. He soon devoted himself to editorial work rather than ministry, but in 1866 the Presbyterians acquired the former Baptist church and after the coming of the railroad replaced it with a brick church. The Presbyterians remained active in education as well as in constructing new churches.

On July 13, 1863, Bishop Talbot left Santa Fe for Taos, riding in a government ambulance. He never returned. For several years occasional Episcopal ser-

---

[2] Josiah Cruickshank Talbot, transcript of diary, New Mexico State Records and Archives, quoted in James M. Stoney, *Lighting the Candle: The Episcopal Church on the Upper Rio Grande* (Santa Fe, 1961), pp. 12-13; Paul Horgan, *Lamy of Santa Fe* (New York, 1975), pp. 296-297.

vices were conducted by the Rev. John Woart, chaplain at Fort Union, and the Rev. J. A. W. LaTourette of Fort Garland. Both forts were three or four days' ride from Santa Fe. In 1868 the General Convention created a missionary district of Colorado, Wyoming, and New Mexico and placed the Rt. Rev. George M. Randall in charge. Randall visited Santa Fe in September, and the Santa Fe *New Mexican* reported that on September 14, 1868, a meeting was held in the hall of the House of Representatives, a part of the Old Palace, at which it was voted to organize a parish of the Protestant Episcopal Church to be known as the Church of the Good Shepherd. The bishop soon returned to his home in Denver, but lay readers conducted services in the home of Col. Frank Bridgeman, the U. S. Paymaster, and then in the Lord Templars Hall facing the Plaza. On his second visit in December 1868 Randall brought with him a gift of a thousand dollars from a member of St. Thomas Church in New York City, payable on condition that the name of the parish be changed to St. Thomas. Naturally the parishioners complied.

The first resident minister to serve St. Thomas was the Rev. John Cornell. He was appointed by the bishop and subsequently confirmed by the vestry. Cornell organized a Sunday School which soon had four teachers and eight "scholars," and he attempted to found a parish school as well. But according to the parish register he tendered his resignation on August 20, 1871, "that being the anniversary of his arrival within this city." The fact that a paragraph of the register has been erased–according to a note by the Senior Warden, Col. Bridgeman, this was done by order of the bishop, because it was "foreign and not pertaining to the history of this church"–may suggest that his departure was not entirely harmonious. After September 1871 services were held in a new chapel on Lincoln Avenue.

The first marriage recorded in the parish register is that of José Manuel Gallegos and Candelaria Montoya. Formerly a Roman Catholic priest, Gallegos is famous for his long-standing controversy with Bishop Lamy. One of several early Catholic clergy in New Mexico who mixed religious and secular lives, Gallegos originally served the parish of St. Felipe de Neri in what is now Old Town, Albuquerque. According to Paul Horgan's colorful description he "was famous for his convivial ways and was regarded as highly intelligent and able, though also as vain and pretentious. He dispensed grape brandy and cakes and changed gold pieces for the rare currency of the province for friends, was a convivial crony of the leading traders and politicians, and had for his housemate a married Mexican woman who had been the mistress of two Mexican officers in turn, by whom she had three children." In due course Lamy had Padre Gallegos suspended. He then served for a time as a delegate to the United States Congress, narrowly defeating Territorial Governor William Carr Lane. His marriage to Candelaria, a widow, was conducted by Chaplain Woart on December 21, 1868, in Gallegos's spacious home on Lincoln Avenue in Santa Fe, the building which now houses the French and French real estate office and the Santacafé restaurant. Witnesses were Robert B. Mitchell, Governor of New Mexico, Col. George W. Getty of the 37th Infantry, and U. S. Marshall John Pratt. A number of the parish's services appear

(2) José M. Gallegos, photo by Frederick Gutekunst, courtesy Museum of New Mexico, Neg. No. 9882.

(3) Padre Gallegos House, Washington Avenue, photo by Arthur Taylor, courtesy Museum of New Mexico, Neg. No. 111932.

to have been held in Gallegos's house, which may have been the chapel on Lincoln Avenue mentioned in some documents, but there is no record that he attempted to officiate at any of them. He died in 1881, supposedly asking for a Roman Catholic priest but without receiving the last rites.[3]

The decade of the 1870s presented difficulties for both the missionary district and the parish. In 1873 John F. Spalding succeeded Bishop Randall. He visited Santa Fe once. Then, in 1874, the General Convention of the Episcopal Church established a smaller and more reasonable jurisdiction for New Mexico and Arizona. William Forbes Adams, a priest from New Orleans, was consecrated bishop, and in February 1875 he arrived in Santa Fe, bringing with him the Rev. Henry Forrester. Adams recorded that they received a hearty welcome; they found a congregation of about forty-five, still meeting in a rented room in a government building. A writer for the *New Mexican* commented that Santa Fe had become the seat of both Catholic and Episcopal dioceses: "there are three Catholic churches and one Protestant Episcopal and one Presbyterian, in each of

---

[3] Horgan, pp. 128, 399; Beatrice Chauvenet, *Holy Faith in Santa Fe* (Santa Fe, 1977), pp. 6-7.

[4] *New Mexican*, February 19, 1875.

which regular services are held every Sunday and on certain week days."[4] Bishop Adams did not remain in Santa Fe. Leaving Forrester behind, he rode on towards Arizona, but he soon heard of the illness of a family member in Louisiana and returned home. He never visited New Mexico again; the strains of life in the rugged west were probably too great for his health.

Forrester was elected rector of St. Thomas, but he soon had to face the fact that there were too few Episcopalians for a viable parish to survive. A number of the original members had been military men or members of their families, and within a few years they "removed" (as the parish register has it) to such locations as Washington, D. C.; Ft. Dodge, Kansas; Charleston, South Carolina; St. Louis; or (within New Mexico) Ft. Wingate, Ft. Bayard, Las Vegas, and Albuquerque. Offerings were also small; in the earliest year recorded (September 1870-September 1871) they amounted to a total of $86.85, of which $20 was allocated for domestic missions. Average attendance then was eight; there were ten communicants, only two of whom were men. So on May 3, 1876, the parish was dissolved and the church reverted to the status of a mission. As the parish register records, "The Mission was under the charge of Rev. H. Forrester until October 26th, 1879, when at his own urgent request he was relieved of the same by Bishop Spalding of Colorado Springs, temporarily in charge of New Mexico and Arizona, and then on a visit to the Mission."[5] A mission committee was appointed, and since the lack of a proper building seemed a severe problem it was shortly converted into a building committee. Both were led by Judge L. B. Prince, whose contributions will shortly engage our attention.

On April 26, 1879, land on Palace Avenue was purchased for $250. Since Prince's committee had raised $363.12 this left $113.12 for a building. Ten businessmen were persuaded to contribute $100 each. Other generous donors included several members of the local Jewish community, probably including the Seligmans, who were prominent merchants. These Jewish friends would eventually be memorialized by a stained glass window depicting the Star of David placed over the entrance to the new structure. Additional fund raising was carried out by the Women of the Church under the leadership of Mrs. John S. Loud. On October 26, 1879, they held a fair which according to the *New Mexican* was a great success, with food, "fancy articles," and art for sale. Entertainment was provided by the string band of the Fourth Cavalry. The cornerstone of the new edifice was laid on September 27, 1881; the new bishop, George K. Dunlop, officiated and

---

[5] Parish Register, pp. 90-91 (removals), 134-135 (offerings), 138 (attendance and communicants), 7 (dissolution of parish).

Judge Prince delivered an address. There was still not a resident priest. With the coming of the railroad, Las Vegas had become a more prosperous town than Santa Fe, and the Rev. David A. Sanford lived there, occasionally traveling to Santa Fe to administer the sacraments and provide pastoral care.

In May 1880 Bishop Spalding had presided at a meeting of members of the mission. Judge Prince, H. C. Baldwin, and W. T. Gaynor were elected delegates to the first convocation of the missionary district of New Mexico and Arizona to be held in Albuquerque a few days later. Then—in the words of the parish register—"a resolution offered by Judge Prince, that the name of the church, if approved by the Bishop, be 'The Church of the Holy Faith,' was unanimously adopted."[6] Prince had taken the name of the state capital, translated into English, for his parish church.

Life in Santa Fe at the time that the Church of the Holy Faith received its name was almost inconceivably more difficult than it was a century later. Before 1881 and the arrival of the Atchison, Topeka, and Santa Fe Railway, under construction from Chicago to California, Santa Fe was one of the most remote and primitive towns in the United States. Its population was about 5,000, mostly Hispanic. The Spanish population had always known the remoteness, but for the Americans who came as merchants, lawyers, Army officers, and political appointees the change was a challenge, and sometimes it was dismaying. Santa Fe was exotic but not artistic. Tourism was virtually unknown; it followed the railroad in the 1890s. Concern for the pueblo Indians and Indian culture was almost nonexistent. The first anthropologist and the first photographer of the pueblos arrived in New Mexico in 1879. Archaeology and interest in the history of New Mexico under Spain scarcely existed before 1890. The names of Adolph F. Bandelier, Frank Hamilton Cushing, Matilda Coxe Stevenson, Charles F. Lummis, Edgar L. Hewett, and Fred Harvey—all great figures in the emerging American fascination with southwest Indian culture—were unknown in 1880. The prevailing progressive idea about Indians everywhere, shaped by Helen Hunt Jackson and the Indian Rights Association, was that native Americans should be rescued from racial oblivion by cutting their hair, educating them, and helping them to become self-supporting farmers.

The city of Santa Fe was then architecturally a collection of crude adobe brick houses, some frontier store fronts around the Plaza, and the new Catholic cathedral. Santa Fe-style architecture, inspired by pueblo mission architecture and the construction of the New Mexico Museum of Fine Arts on the corner of

---

[6] Parish Register, p. 7; cf. Chauvenet, pp. 9-12.

the Plaza in 1917, was not even a glint in any man's eye in 1880. Public health in the city was dismal and growing worse. This was the decade in which American medicine discovered that the high, dry climates of Colorado Springs and the Rocky Mountains south of it were beneficial for tubercular patients from the crowded, damp cities of the East. After 1881 nearly every transcontinental passenger train left off a few patients at Las Vegas, Lamy, or Albuquerque, some of them to take up residence in Santa Fe or the tent city at Sunmount, out toward the present-day suburb of El Dorado. Many "lungers" were healed, but along the way they also spread tuberculosis in Santa Fe, where public health standards were almost non-existent, privies were located in backyards side by side with private wells, and raw sewage ran down Water Street into the Santa Fe River. Americans in those days did not retire to Santa Fe except to cope with respiratory afflictions. In some cases the "Anglos" came to Santa Fe on federal government duty, and when their service was complete, they returned or "retired" to Pennsylvania or New York or wherever they had come from.

By the end of the decade there was a more positive side to Santa Fe. Commenting on the situation in October 1889, a writer for the *New Mexican* argued that it had "more advantages for a residence city than any other town in the southwest."

(4) Original church of the Holy Faith and rectory, photograph about 1912, courtesy Museum of New Mexico, Neg. No. 61359.

We have an unequaled diversity of views here. Eight mountain ranges clothed with foliage of the richest hues encircle our beautiful plain. There are nearer hills, can[y]ons, bluffs and table lands, and a mountain stream winding through these and down a broadening valley. From the hill sides we look upon stately public buildings, a massive cathedral and hospital, elegant chapels, churches, colleges, acade-

(5) Church of the Holy Faith and rectory, photograph taken about 1900 from site of Fort Marcy, copy in church office. The church is the building on the left.

(6) Interior of original church, photograph courtesy Museum of New Mexico, Neg. No. 40292.

mies and industrial schools, a spacious sanatarium and a graceful and capacious hotel prominent among other structures. Here are ancient buildings and modern in curious contrast for the sight seer. Our mercantile houses are piled with goods daily distributed by two railroads over the territory. The narrow business streets are often crowded with queer looking Mexican teams, through which the great American transfer wagons find difficult passage. At this season and in spring are seen cavalcades of well painted and gayly dressed Navajoes with a score or two of horses, or the poorer but wiser Apaches, bringing their children to school. Always the somber looking Pueblo stands dreamily looking upon American activities as dumb as the ever present burro under his loads of wood, fruit and grain.[7]

---

[7] *New Mexican*, October 8, 1889, quoted in Oliver La Farge, *Santa Fe: The Autobiography of a Southwest Town* (Norman, Oklahoma, 1959), p. 134.

This was the context in which the tiny parish of the Holy Faith struggled before the First World War: it served the few Episcopalians who lived, often of necessity rather than from birth or preference, in a beautiful but crude town with few amenities.

Little is known about the construction of Holy Faith's new building, which remains as the nave of the present church. The architectural style may be characterized as folk Gothic, perhaps a simplified version of the thirteenth-century Early English style seen in many English cathedrals and parish churches. According to the New Mexico historian Myra Ellen Jenkins, who was herself a communicant, the stone cutting and masonry were the work of her grandfather, Levi Ackroyd, an immigrant from England who lived in Denver. Judge Prince had been impressed with his abilities and persuaded him and his four brothers to do the construction "for a reasonable price." Originally the windows were plain glass, and it is said that the chancel window had no glass at all but was covered by a red curtain. Benches and some other furniture, together with a reed organ, were brought from the room where the church had been meeting. Mrs. Prince paid for the front doors. A short history of the parish written some years later by Mrs. R. J. Palen tells us that the Rev. E. W. Meany, who served Holy Faith from 1892 to 1894, paid for the altar, which he designed himself, and raised money for "a beautiful churchly red carpet to cover the entire church, which he ordered from England. The Bishop's chair, the Priest's seats, credence table, prayer desk, and lectern were given by Mrs. J. G. Palen in memory of her husband who had died and was buried there [i.e. near the altar]. Through the influence of Mr. Meany the money to set off the choir on one side and make a vestry room on the other was raised by Mrs. T. B. Catron, at that time a member of the choir."[8] These furnishings were supplemented by the gifts of outsiders. As the parish register recorded,

> the following gifts were received by the mission: four sets of richly
> embroidered markers from the Misses Fairchild of Madison, Wis.;
> a hymn board, from Capt. Wm. Paulding U.S.A.; a book of altar
> services and a large prayer book from Sister Gertrude of New York,
> also an altar book rest from Sister Gertrude. This last gift [was]
> given on condition that if it should be replaced by another book rest
> so that it goes into disuse, it shall be returned to the donor to be
> disposed of at her discretion.

---

[8] Mrs. R. J. Palen, history of the early years of Holy Faith, typescript in parish archives.

When properly fitted up the building had a seating capacity of 200. At first there was no furnace, merely two large stoves whose ventilating pipes ran through the top of the windows, but about 1908 the Women of the Church, now organized as the Holy Faith Guild, paid for the installation of a proper chimney.[9]

The first service of the Church of the Holy Faith in its new building was held on August 6, 1882. A permanent Episcopal presence in Santa Fe seemed assured.

---

[9] Parish Register, p. 6; Chauvenet, 24-25.

2. Church and State, 1899-1917

One of the remarkable aspects of the early years of the Church of the Holy Faith is the close relationship between the mission or parish and the civic and political life of the territory of New Mexico. Many of the same leaders served both church and state.

As we have seen, the establishment of the Church of the Holy Faith was more the work of a layman, L. Bradford Prince, than of any single member of the clergy. Prince had been born in Flushing, New York, on July 3, 1840. He was a descendant of Governor William Bradford of Plymouth, author of the renowned history of Plymouth Plantation; the relationship was memorialized in Prince's Christian name. (The "L." stood for LeBaron, a name he never used.) Both his great-grandfather and his grandfather had been governors of Rhode Island. According to a memorial address given to the Historical Society of New Mexico by its vice-president, Frank W. Clancy, following Prince's death in 1922, Prince had been interested in political activities while still a boy. Even before his graduation from Columbia Law School he had published a book, *E Pluribus Unum, or American Nationality*, which reviewed the country's government from colonial times through the Articles of Confederation and the adoption of the Constitution.

Prince's political career had begun in New York in 1871, when he was elected to the state legislature. This was something of an achievement, for he had already formed his life-long attachment to the Republican party and was running in a strongly Democratic district. He fought against political corruption and helped break the power of Tammany Hall. There appear to have been several reasons for his move to the southwest. He disliked the autocratic domination of New York politics by Roscoe Conkling and determined to make his mark in another part of

(7) L. Bradford Prince, photo courtesy Museum of New Mexico, Neg. No. 50444.

(8) Mary C. Prince (Mrs. L. Bradford Prince), photo by Herman Wunder Studio, courtesy Museum of New Mexico, Neg. No. 10354.

the country. He was also fascinated by what he heard of New Mexico and its people. In 1878 President Rutherford B. Hayes offered to appoint him governor of Idaho, but Prince declined the position. According to one story he was offended by a delegate from the Idaho territory who received him without shoes and perhaps generally without due respect. Then, later in the same year, the President named him chief justice of New Mexico. He arrived in Santa Fe that winter.[1]

Prince's career as chief justice was stormy and he served only four years, resigning in 1882. Frank Clancy, who was his clerk throughout most of this period, left an interesting characterization of his style. "His only fault as a judge, if it were a fault, was in the excessive amount of work which he performed and imposed upon the members of the bar and state officers. [When holding court at Las Vegas] he opened court at 8 in the morning, adjourned from 12 to 1 to permit the eating of a mid-day meal, and from 6 to 7 for supper, and never stopped before 11 at night. He was always alert, and apparently untired, but everyone else was worn out."[2] During his years as a judge Prince prepared a compilation of the laws of New Mexico—it was said that he did the work while on the train for one of his visits to New York. After leaving the bench Prince practiced law in Santa Fe, becoming involved especially in land grant claims. In 1889 President Benjamin Harrison appointed him Governor of New Mexico. Among his chief concerns was the establishment of public schools throughout the territory. During his four years in office he entertained splendidly in the Governor's Palace but continued to live in his own home in Prince Plaza, halfway between the Palace and the Episcopal church, now the home of the Shed restaurant. After his term as Governor Prince was active as a historian; he wrote a history of New Mexico, together with a shortened version intended for students, a classic study of *Spanish Mission Churches of New Mexico* (1915),[3] and many articles, some of

---

[1] For biographical information about Prince see Frank W. Clancy, "In Memory of L. Bradford Prince," a pamphlet published by the Historical Society of New Mexico, No. 25, 1923, and Beatrice Chauvenet, *Holy Faith in Santa Fe* (Santa Fe, 1977), pp. 13-15. Prince's papers are in the New Mexico State Archives, Accession No. 1959-174. The *New Mexican* had supported Col. J. W. Dyer for appointment as governor but was "well satisfied now that the choice has been made." *New Mexican*, April 2, 1889, quoted in Oliver La Farge, *Santa Fe: The Autobiography of a Southwestern Town* (Norman, Oklahoma, 1959), pp. 135-36.

[2] Clancy, p. 5.

[3] The book was reprinted in 1977 by the Rio Grande Press with a number of illustrations.

which dealt with the Episcopal church. Clancy's memorial noted that Prince was a total abstainer from alcohol, including wine, "but he never said a word or had a thought of criticism of those whose habits of life were different from his own." His activities in dealing with land grants involved him in what came to be known as the Santa Fe Ring, of which more will be said later.

As a lay reader (one of only five in the district) Prince often conducted services at Holy Faith when there was no resident priest. Between 1882 and 1890 the Rev. E. W. Meany, who had come to New Mexico from Florida, was in change of the parish, but he was often absent to work in Lamy, Cerrillos, Watrous, or Albuquerque. According to the parish register "Rev. Meaney removed to Prescott [Arizona] about Nov. 1, 1890. Rev. T. J. Glyn deacon, officiated Feb. 15, 22, & Mch. 1, 1891; took charge of the Mission Mch. 26; died May 20th 1891, of consumption. During the year from Nov. 1, 1890, to Nov. 1, 1891, Bishop Kendrick officiated about 10 times; Rev. Beauchamp of Central New York, once; Gov. Prince, as lay reader, 27 times." In November 1891 another deacon, the Rev. Sanderson H. S. Ilderton, was appointed minister in charge, but he too died of consumption within a few months. One of the stained glass windows in the church memorializes his brief ministry. During 1892 the Rev. George H. Mueller of Minnesota officiated from May to November. "From then till May 1893 services were sustained by L. B. Prince, lay reader, with occasional visits from the bishop." The rapid turn-over of clergy continued until the end of the century, with Albert C. Monk, Frederick T. Bennett, Hale Townsend, J. L. Gay, and Edward Lyman Eustice serving terms of two years or less. Prince advised many of them as senior warden. A non-Episcopalian interviewed by Beatrice Chauvenet said that "he ran the Episcopal Church, and he always opposed raising the minister's salary because he didn't want any cleric to grow more powerful in the church than himself."[4]

Prince was one of the guiding spirits of the missionary district as well as the church in Santa Fe. We have noted his attendance at the first Convocation in 1880, at which time he was appointed Chancellor of the district, an office which he held for the remaining forty-two years of his life. As Bishop James M. Stoney later wrote, "There were other faithful laymen in the infancy of the diocese. . . . But somehow, the Hon. L. Bradford Prince's name seemed always on the list, even at the primary convocation of the Missionary District of New Mexico where he was the only layman outside of the local congregation who put in an appear-

---

[4] Chauvenet, p. 15.

(9) Governor Prince's reception room, Palace of the Governors, where early meetings of the church took place, photograph taken February 14, 1893, by Thomas J. Curran, courtesy Museum of New Mexico, Neg. No. 16658.

ance."[5] His spirituality is perhaps testified to by his collection of "Devotionals," small booklets printed in Spanish during the later 1700s, examples of which are a "Novena a la Santisima Virgen Maria de Guadalupe" (1797) and "Exorcismo a los Moribundos" (1787).[6]

Prince married twice. In 1879 he wed a young woman from New York, Hattie Estelle Childs, but she died within months of coming to Santa Fe, succumbing to pneumonia which she contracted while traveling to Denver on the new train promoted by Prince and some of his friends. She is memorialized at Holy Faith by a stained glass window—the one nearest the sacristy—which depicts a crimson-robed saint with a palm frond in her hand and a lamb at her feet. In 1881 Prince married his second wife, Mary C. Beardsley of Oswego, New York. She outlived him, helped host many social and civic events, was active at Holy

[5] James M. Stoney, *Lighting the Candle: The Episcopal Church on the Upper Rio Grande* (Santa Fe, 1961), p. 56.

[6] L. Bradford Prince Papers, Box 14022, Folders 1-7, New Mexico State Archives. The examples are from Folder 1.

Faith, and gave Prince a son, William, baptized at the home of his parents on December 14, 1882. At the end of his life Prince returned to New York and died at his home on Long Island December 8, 1922. His wife Mary died there on Christmas Day, 1925. William Prince remained in Santa Fe and married Florence Howland; they had three sons and a daughter, Louise, an invalid who continued to live in the family home on Palace Avenue for many years.

†

One of Prince's associates in both church and state was Thomas Benton Catron. Born in Missouri in 1840, Catron graduated from the University of Missouri and served in the Confederate army during the Civil War. He came to New Mexico in 1866. The following year he was admitted to the bar and married Julia A. Walz, who come from Mankato, Minnesota. Their sons John Walz, Charles Christopher, Thomas B., and Fletcher were baptized at Holy Faith and the family is listed in the first parish register; Julia sang in the choir. Although he had been a Democrat in Missouri, Catron soon realized that the Republicans were going to be in power in New Mexico as long as there was a Republican administration in Washington and so joined Judge Prince's party. Characterized by R. E. Twitchell as possessing great strength of character but having "as many enemies as friends" and by E. Donald Kaye as being "very smart and very ambitious," he was appointed Attorney General of the territory in 1869. In 1912, at the first session of the legislature after New Mexico achieved statehood, Catron was elected to the United States Senate. He was one of the owners of the First National Bank in Santa Fe and also controlled the weekly *New Mexican*. It is said that at one time Catron owned or had an interest in more land than anyone else in the United States, perhaps six million acres. He is generally thought to have been the leader of the so-called Santa Fe Ring, a Republican group that dominated territorial land and politics. The Ring was involved in the notorius Lincoln County War, a controversy which led to at least one murder and the fame of Billy the Kid. In 1911 Bronson Cutting (of whom more later) wrote that Catron was "the boss of the territory . . . and probably the most unscrupulous man in the Southwest," while a draft circular prepared by the Democratic Auxiliary Committee in 1892 claimed that he "has no sympathy with progressive men and modern methods, and has steadily opposed the cutting up of large [land] grants into convenient homes for farmers and others."[7]

---

[7] L. Bradford Prince Papers, Box 14019, Folder 20, New Mexico State Archives.

(10) Thomas B. Catron, photograph courtesy Museum of New Mexico, Neg. No. 50364.

The friendship between the Catrons and Princes is testified to by an undated letter from Mrs. Catron to Mr. Prince. Writing from Berlin, she suggested that some post cards of Santa Fe should be made for sale at the Omaha Exposition of 1906–"beautiful souvenir postal cards . . . are the rage now in this part of the world." She concluded, "How are Mrs. Prince and Willie? Give them my love and best wishes."[8] Catron's office was upstairs in the Catron Building which he erected on the east side of the Plaza, with large windows overlooking the Governor's Palace; the space is now occupied by the Dewey art gallery. T. B. Catron died in 1921. A number of his descendants remain in Santa Fe but most are no longer members of the Episcopal church.[9]

Two men who served with Bradford Prince on the Holy Faith building committee were William G. Ritch and William W. Griffin. Ritch had been born in New York state in 1830. While still young he moved to Michigan and then to Wisconsin; he served in a Wisconsin regiment during the Civil War and shortly thereafter became editor and owner of a Wisconsin newspaper. Like many others, he moved to New Mexico in the hope that the dry climate would improve his health. In 1873 President Ulysses S. Grant named him Secretary of the Territory, an office which he held for a number of years. He later served as Governor. His children Nellie, Emma, and Watson are listed as family members in the first Holy Faith register. Ritch is remembered for his work in establishing the Historical Society of New Mexico. Founded in 1860, it had become moribund shortly thereafter but was resurrected and reorganized with Ritch as its president in 1880. In his memorial to Bradford Prince, Frank Clancy described Ritch as a man who combined imagination with high executive ability. The Society's early collections of Indian, Mexican, Spanish, and American objects were gathered largely through his initiative. Following his death in 1904 Prince succeeded him as President of the Historical Society.[10]

Griffin was born in 1831.[11] A native of West Virginia, it is said that he made his way to New Mexico partly on foot. He became a clerk in the U.S. Quartermaster's office and was later employed as collector of internal revenue,

---

[8] L. Bradford Prince Papers, Box 14019, Folder 20, New Mexico State Archives.

[9] There is a biography of Catron: Victor Westphall, *Thomas Benton Catron and His Era* (Tucson, 1973). I am grateful to Donald Kaye for sharing with me his paper on Catron and the Lincoln County War, as well as other comments and information. Chauvenet mentions Catron, p. 19.

[10] Clancy, p. 10; Chauvenet, p. 16.

[11] Chauvenet, p. 15, says 1830, but the first parish register, p. 60, gives August 27, 1831. Rather surprisingly, Griffin was not baptized until December 3, 1889, although he had been active in the church much earlier.

then (utilizing his training as a civil engineer) as a government surveyor. Like Catron, he was part owner of the First National Bank, which he eventually served as President. He was one of several members of Holy Faith who were active Masons and was the first Grand Master of the Grand Lodge of the territory. His wife, Jennie M. Miller, came to Santa Fe from Missouri. Meetings of the Episcopal mission were sometimes held at their home close to the site of the Holy Faith building, and one of the stained glass windows installed in the new church, displaying flower medallions topped by a cross, crown, and dove, was given by Jennie Griffin in memory of her parents. The Griffins' seven children are listed in the first church register. Two died young; both Charles (aged 13) and Viola (aged 6) were stricken by diphtheria during the summer of 1892.[12]

Of greater importance in the life of the parish were members of the Palen family. The progenitor, Joseph P. Palen, had been born in New York state in 1812 and educated at Amherst and Harvard. He preceded Prince as chief justice of the territory of New Mexico, serving from 1869 until his death in 1875. His son, Rufus James Palen, had also been born in New York state—the year was 1843— and accompanied Joseph to New Mexico after studying law at the University of Michigan and serving as a major in the Union army. For a time he served as his father's law clerk; later he became a banker, following Griffin as President of the First National Bank. A staunch Republican, he also served several terms as treasurer of the territory. In addition to being a vestryman and treasurer of Holy Faith, he was president of the New Mexico Bankers' Association and an active member of the Santa Fe Society of the Archaeological Institute of America.

In 1887 Rufus Palen married Ellen Seager Webbe, the daughter of an Episcopal bishop. On a crucial occasion Ellen provided hospitality to Bishop John F. Spalding. Her account is colorful.

> New Mexico had not yet learned to honor her bishops, [as] was shown by [Spalding's] experience in Silver City. Having finished the evening service and put his robes in his suitcase, he found himself entirely alone in the church. No one offered to carry his bag or escort him to his hotel. The streets were dark and he soon left the sidewalk, rolled down an embankment and found himself near the window of a house on a lower street. He attracted attention and was helped to the hotel with a broken wrist . . . He wrote Judge Prince that he would stop in Santa Fe over the next Sunday provided he

---

[12] Parish Register 1, p. 120; Chauvenet, p. 16, does not list Viola.

(11) Rufus J. Palen, photo courtesy Museum of New Mexico, Neg. No. 50439.

(12) Mrs. Rufus J. Palen, photo courtesy Museum of New Mexico, Neg. No. 110852.

could stop at a private home. With his broken arm he could not go to a hotel. I had my little six or seven month old baby, but I said he could come to me, which he did.[13]

As Chauvenet notes, the baby was their daughter Caryl. In 1904 she was married at Holy Faith, but she died in 1912. Her parents never recovered from the loss. Rufus's health declined, and he died in 1916 at the age of 73. His obituary commented that "not since the funeral of the late Archbishop J. B. Lamy has Santa Fe witnessed so general and heartfelt a demonstration of sorrow as on the sunny, balmy March afternoon when the mortal remains of Major Palen were borne to their last resting place." Holy Faith was too small to hold all those who wished to attend. Among the honorary pallbearers were Dr. W. S. Harroun, Bronson Cutting, Arthur and James Seligman, and L. Bradford Prince.[14] Ellen Palen remained active in the life of the church until her own death in 1927. She was one of the early secretaries of the Woman's Auxiliary to the National Council and later a vice-president. The church's parish house, Palen Hall, is named in memory of Caryl.

Two more churchmen who were prominent in politics were William T. Thornton and Edward L. Bartlett. Thornton served as governor and was as controversial as T. B. Catron, while Bartlett was solicitor general for many years. One of the windows in the nave of Holy Faith is a memorial to the Bartletts, paid for by the sale of his personal jewelry and installed under the supervision of Mrs. Palen.[15]

---

[13] Mrs. Palen's short history of the early years of Holy Faith is among the Bradford Prince papers in the state archives; there is a typed copy in the church archives. This passage is quoted in Chauvenet, pp. 10-11. See also pp. 19-20.

[14] Obituary from *Old Santa Fe*, Vol. III, No. 10, April 1916.

[15] See Chauvenet, pp. 17-19 and 20-22.

(13) William T. Thornton, photo courtesy Museum of New Mexico, Neg. No. 50530.

(14) Mrs. William T. Thornton, photo courtesy Museum of New Mexico, Neg. No. 50532.

CHURCH AND STATE, 1899-1917

3. From Mission to Parish, 1899-1917

The early years of the twentieth century continued to be difficult for Holy Faith. Clergy still served relatively short terms. As we have seen, The Rev. Edward L. Eustis was priest-in-charge from 1899 to 1901. His successor, Walter R. Dye, was in place from 1901 to 1909, but his successors, Frederick W. Pratt and James Mythen, remained less than a year each.

Eustis's years saw a number of improvements. When the Convocation of the district met at Holy Faith in May 1900 a chalice and paten, described in the parish register as "handsome," were used for the first time; they were gifts of St. John's parish in Germantown, Pennsylvania. A bread box and a pair of cruets were soon added, the cruets being given partly by Caryl Palen. On March 10, 1901, a two-manual pipe organ was dedicated. It had been made by Hook and Hastings of Boston, one of the leading organ builders of the day, and its cost, $1000, was "secured through the efforts of the Ladies Guild."[1] Hook and Hastings organs are still cherished by historic organ enthusiasts, and it is a pity that the instrument has not been retained at Holy Faith, perhaps for use in the chapel. Originally the organ was pumped by hand. Beatrice Chauvenet knew Alfred Wiley, a vestryman who as a boy had been paid $1.50 a month for pumping during choir practice and the 11:00 service; when an evening service was added he received an additional sixty cents. During Mr. Eustis's ministry a quartet was organized to serve as the choir. Since many members of Holy Faith were also Masons, the group often sang at the Masonic Temple as well as the church. The first organist was Eustis's sister-in-law, Mary Roberta Van Stone.[2]

---

[1] Parish Register 2, p. 7.
[2] Beatrice Chauvenet, *Holy Faith in Santa Fe* (Santa Fe, 1977), pp. 32-34.

Walter Dye had come to the Southwest because of his wife's poor health, and the couple returned to Mississippi in September 1909, following her recovery. Frederick Pratt, a missionary at large in New Mexico, served only in a temporary capacity pending the appointment of a presbyter. He later worked in Clovis and Roswell. James Mythen was only a deacon, not a priest, but he was popular with the people of Holy Faith. Jimmie, as he was called, organized Santa Fe's first Boy Scout troop and held church picnics at Monument Rock in the Santa Fe canyon. It was he who first had the idea of a Santa Fe fiesta, and the proposal was promoted by his friends James and Ruth Seligman. As Mrs. Seligman said when interviewed in 1963,

> the real idea of a town fiesta came from the Episcopal minister named James Mythen—a very brilliant young man who preached the most marvelous sermons.... Mr. Mythen got to talking to us and he said, "You know, I don't see why Santa Fe doesn't have some yearly historical event as they do in New Orleans at Mardi Gras. Santa Fe is so full of history." So Jim and I were very much interested, and a few days later after Mr. Mythen left [to return east], Jim asked a few men to come up to the house. We sat around our dining table, and Jim suggested that one of the best things to start with would be the reconquest by De Vargas.... That's the way it started. It was Jimmy Mythen's idea to have some historical event and Jim Seligman's idea to have De Vargas.[3]

James Seligman and his brother Arthur, later mayor of Santa Fe and governor of New Mexico, were sons of the Jewish merchant Bernard Seligman and his wife Frances Nusbaum. Both James and Arthur married Episcopalians. James's wife Ruth Ritchie was baptized at Holy Faith in 1911, as were her children Morton (aged 15) and Beatrice (aged 12). Richie Harris Seligman, later Mrs. March, was confirmed in 1911. The religious views of the brothers remained ambiguous. It does not appear that there was a funeral at Holy Faith when Arthur died in 1933, shortly after his re-election as governor, but the Episcopal service for the dead was read in the House of Representatives. The Seligman's were Democrats, and thus political rivals of the Princes and Catrons.[4]

A rectory had been built in 1893 on land behind the church. Described as a two-story Victorian-style home, it was largely paid for by the Guild, which raised

---

[3] Quoted in Chris Wilson, *The Myth of Santa Fe* (Albuquerque, 1997), pp. 196-97.

[4] Henry J. Tobias, *A History of the Jews in New Mexico* (Albuquerque, 1990), pp.113-114, 160; Parish Register 3, pp. 136, 156, 158.

about $1600 under the leadership of Mary Prince. An additional $800 was borrowed by the Church Building Commission. The house was rented out for $25 a month until the debt was cleared, and the rectory was not available to a clergyman until 1899.[5] Ellen Palen described it as being very comfortable and pretty, with "a good-sized sitting or living room; very nice study; dining-room, hall, kitchen and a great deal of pantry room on the first floor. Three large bedrooms, bath, linen closet and porch on the second floor."[6]

The clergy must have welcomed this residence, but they were poorly paid. The salary was about $500 out of a church budget which ran between $700 and $800 a year. Other expenses included the cost of music (purchased from the publishers Lyon and Healey) and communion wine, as well as gifts to the Domestic and Foreign Missionary Society and (interestingly) for "work among the Jews." Offerings on Easter Day 1900 amounted to $48, of which only $29 was for general expenses; there might have been more had it not been a "very stormy day."[7]

There continued to be a rapid turn-over of church members. The list of families in the second parish register records that many had "removed" or "gone away." Others died. The third register, which goes down to 1918, refers to a number of men serving in the army. The register of burials is a poignant reminder of the shortness of life common during pioneer days. One infant boy lived only a day. Other children died at the ages of 5, 8, 10½, and 15 months. Even adults were carried off in their twenties and thirties. The causes of death were listed as pneumonia, dysentery, consumption, cancer, paralysis, diarrhea, tuberculosis, peritonitis, heart disease, and "mountain fever." There is also one case of a gunshot wound and two of blood poisoning. Only a few, like the Rev. J. L. Gay, died of "old age" (he was 94, as his shaky handwriting in the parish register suggests). It is interesting to see that a "colored Methodist" woman and three American Indians, one a Shoshone who was the son of "Piute Charlie," were among those who had funerals at Holy Faith. Six Apache girls had been baptized in 1895, one of their sponsors being "Mr. Goulette, a Sioux Indian." There are very few Hispanic names on the lists of communicants; they include Lena and Carolyn Delgado, Isadora Baca, and Lena Montoya, a baby. Among the prominent communicants were Henry and Anna Kaune, together with their daughters Alice and Felicitas, Dr. and Mrs. William S. Harroun, and Nellie Marian Nusbaum.[8]

---

[5] Parish Registry 1, p. 8.
[6] Chauvenet, p. 31.
[7] Parish Register 2, pp. 122-123.
[8] Parish Register 2, pp. 10-26, 114-119; Parish Register 3, pp. 140-176.

Internal dissension also plagued the mission. Initially these disputes involved the Princes and the Palens–the men became rivals in the church and their wives led factions in the Woman's Guild. Affairs were complicated by the arrival of Bronson Murray Cutting. The descendant of an Anglican priest who had migrated to America in the eighteenth century and several generations of New York lawyers, Cutting had left his studies at Harvard in 1911 and come to New Mexico in the hope of curing his tuberculosis. He immediately became a communicant of Holy Faith. In 1912 he acquired ownership of the *New Mexican*, the territory's oldest newspaper, and served as its editor. His political views were more liberal than those of the Republican leaders; he has been credited with encouraging Hispanics to take part in state government. He was appointed to the United States Senate in 1927 to fill a vacancy, duly elected in 1928, and reelected in 1934, but he died in a plane crash in 1935.

Elected a warden of Holy Faith, Cutting quarreled with Prince in 1911 over the proposal that the mission should seek parish status. Initially Prince was opposed–he was happy enough to accept the financial support being provided by the Church Mission Board—while Cutting and Mythen, the deacon in charge, believed that the church was now able to support itself. An advantage of parish status was that the church could call its own rector rather than accepting clergy named by the bishop. Cutting's biographer, drawing on the senator's papers, described a meeting at which everybody was "shouting, stamping and pounding on the table at once." The vast majority of the congregation shared Cutting's view; Prince, he said, quickly alienated most of the congregation with his belligerence. But Prince had the support of Bishop Kendrick, who dismissed Mythen just as he was about to leave on a vacation—the deacon submitted his resignation at Easter 1911. For some reason, possibly the influence of the bishop, Prince soon changed his mind and agreed to support parish status. On the evening of May 31 the bishop "gave notice of the organization of [the] parish" and ordered the election of vestrymen. Even then, however, "Cutting, along with most other members, was appalled by but unable to restrain L. Bradford Prince, who used highhanded tactics to maintain prominence in church affairs."[9] Perhaps it was inevitable that one who had given so much of his life to the church should seek to fix its course.

It took some time to find a new rector. For several months the Rev. M. J.

[9] Richard Lowitt, *Bronson M. Cutting, Progresssive Politician* (Albuquerque, 1992), pp.29-31, 51; Chauvenet, pp. 35-36. See also Oliver La Farge, *Santa Fe: The Autobiography of a Southwestern Town* (Norman, Oklahoma, 1956), esp. pp. 336-39, 350.

(15) U. S. Senator Bronson Cutting meeting with President-elect Franklin D. Roosevelt at Warm Springs, Georgia, December 5, 1932, photo courtesy Museum of New Mexico, Neg. No.138126.

Villareal conducted services. One of the "Old Catholics" from France, he was a friend of both Prince and Bishop Kendrick and was said to be a charming man, but his English was not adequate for ministry in an English-speaking parish; recognizing this, Kendrick had paid him a meager stipend out of his own pocket rather than from church funds. In the Fall of 1911 the Rev. John Withers Heal was called by the vestry to serve for six months as a temporary *locum tenens*. He returned to Colorado in May. The Rev. Leonidas W. Smith, a missionary at the Church of the Good Shepherd in Silver City, was then asked to fill the vacancy. Evidently apprensive about becoming rector, at his own request he came as *locum tenens* for only a month and then went to Alaska. Bradford Prince again led the services in June and July, but Smith had proved himself popular and was asked to return. As he wrote in the parish register, on August 2, 1912, "the Rev. Leonidas W. Smith, having accepted the call to the Parish of the Holy Faith, unanimously extended by the Vestry, arrived at Santa Fe and began his services as rector, being

(16) Rev. Leonidas W. Smith, photo from the Church of Holy Faith parish archives, Box II.16.

the first Rector of the Parish."[10]

Smith served until 1917. As keeper of the parish register he obviously enjoyed providing details of his activities and accomplishments. It is worth quoting
them to gain a sense of his style as well as his work.

Sept. 1912. Appointed Scout Master. Served with Santa Fe Boy Scouts two years.

1913, Oct. Founded and organized (with approval of the Rt. Rev. Daniel S. Tuttle,
Acting Bishop of the District), St. Stephen's Mission, Española, N.M.

Aug. 23, 1913. Married Miss Corinna Gertrude Hanes at Sonora, Ohio.

Oct. 1913. Initiated and appointed Chaplain, B.P.O.E. [Elks Club] of Santa Fe.

1913. Appointed by the Rt. Rev. Cameron Mann, Acting Bishop, delegate to the
Council of the 7th Department at Austin, Texas, and served.

1913. Elected Chaplain of the first Senate of the State of New Mexico, and
served.

1914. Appointed by the Rt. Rev. Frederick B. Howden, D.D., Registrar of the
District. Appointed member of the Council.

1914. Appointed Chaplain to the Santa Fe Branch of the Actors' Church Alli-
ance.

1914. Appointed by the bishop as official correspondent for the District.

1914. Appointed Missionary-in-charge of Holy Apostles' Mission, Taos, N.M.,
and of St. Alban's Mission, Estancia, N.M.

Nov. 1914. Began building operations for the new St. Stephen's Church, Española,
N.M. Guild organized.

March 2, 1915. St. Stephen's Church, Española, N.M. dedicated by the Rt. Rev.
Frederick B. Howden, D.D. Sunday School organized.

Oct. 1915. Appointed editor and manager of The New Mexico Churchman.
Served to Oct. 1917.

July 14, 1917. St. Stephen's Church meets final payment on the new Church at
that point, except the "Grant" of $300 promised by the American Church
Building Fund Commission.

Sept. 15, 1917. The Rev. L. W. Smith, rector, accepts appointment as Archdeacon of the Diocese of Kansas.

Oct. 2, 1917. At a special meeting of the wardens and vestrymen, the rector
tenders his resignation, the same to take effect Oct. 10, 1917.

Oct. 10, 1917. Rev. Leonidas W. Smith and family leave for Topeka, Kansas.[11]

---

[10] Parish Register 3, pp. 6-7.
[11] Parish Register 3, pp. 7-9.

A number of "notable improvements" made between 1913 and 1917 are listed in the register. A new lectern was installed as a memorial to Bishop Kendrick. Then a processional cross was introduced, and a vested choir sang for the first time at Holy Faith on Easter Day 1914. The organ was tuned and an electric blower was installed, the cost of $150 being borne by Women's Guild. In 1917 the Girls' Friendly Society paid for kneeling benches. Smith no doubt deserved much of the credit for these changes; he had served the church well.

The list of baptisms for these years is interesting because it reveals how many families were newcomers to Santa Fe. Places of birth include Española, Aztec, Farmington, Chama, Lamy, Portales, Las Cruces, Las Vegas, Santa Rosa, and Albuquerque in New Mexico; Chicago, Kansas City, Brooklyn, and Washington, D.C.; towns in Iowa, Colorado, Minnesota, Wisconsin, Kansas, Nebraska, South Dakota, Virginia, Illinois, Texas, and Arizona; and London, Ontario. Among those christened were two grandchildren of L. Bradford Prince (Louise LeBaron and William Raymond) and Leonidas Smith's own daughter Virginia Gertrude.[12] Those confirmed included persons baptized in the Congregational, Methodist, Presbyterian, Baptist, Campbellite, and Roman Catholic churches as well as Episcopalians. Each annual group of confirmands numbered about ten.[13]

---

[12] Parish Register 3, pp. 54-75.
[13] Parish Register 3, pp. 136-38.

4. The Mellowing Years, 1918-1935

The period from 1918 to 1936 was a time of unusual stability at Holy Faith. There was a single rector, Walter S. Trowbridge, and a single bishop, Frederick B. Howden. The Rev. Mr. Trowbridge had come to New Mexico in 1917 from the cathedral at Michigan City, Indiana, to be archdeacon of the missionary district. He took up his work at Holy Faith in January 1918, soon after the departure of Leonidas Smith. Trowbridge's first wife, Charlotte Frances, died shortly after arriving in Santa Fe. She is memorialized in a stained glass window at the southeast corner of the church; made by the distinguished Philadelphia firm of Willet and given by her brothers, it depicts St. Hilda, the great seventh-century abbess of Whitby, with a goose at her feet. Howden had been born in New York and served churches there and in Michigan, Maryland, and Washington, D.C., before being elected Missionary Bishop of New Mexico and Southwest Texas in 1913. As we will see, Trowbridge left Santa Fe in 1935. The bishop died in 1940. James Stoney referred to the last period of Howden's bishopric as "the mellowing years"; the term may equally well be applied to Holy Faith during the decades of Trowbridge's ministry.[1]

This was a relatively quiet era in Santa Fe. The population remained small and stable: in 1936 the county had fewer than 30,000 inhabitants. The stability extended to the parish and its officers as well.[2] Dr. W. S. Harroun served as senior warden during the first two years of Trowbridge's tenure. A graduate of the University of Michigan and Georgetown Medical School, he had been a Civil War

---

[1] James M. Stoney, *Lighting the Candle: The Episcopal Church on the Upper Rio Grande* (Santa Fe, 1961), p. 137. Howden's career is described on pp. 219-220.

[2] Unless otherwise attributed all information in this chapter is taken from files of annual reports in the parish archives.

(17) Palen Hall, photo ca. 1976 by Arthur Taylor, courtesy Museum of New Mexico, Neg. No. 117109.

surgeon and Professor of Pulmonary Diseases at Rush Medical College before moving to Santa Fe in 1881, hoping to improve his wife's health.[3] He was succeeded in 1920 by Charles B. Barker, an attorney specializing in public law and mining law, who remained in office until the rector's departure. Bronson M.

---

[3] His wife, Mary, was the daughter of Dr. Douglas Houghton, State Geologist of Michigan. She taught herself Spanish and translated some Spanish folk tales after moving to New Mexico. In 1891 she helped found the Fifteen Club, a literary society for ladies, which is the oldest ladies' organization in the state and is still flourishing today. I am grateful to their relative Dorothy Harroun for providing biographical information about the family.

(18) Map of Santa Fe in 1928, from Santa Fe New Mexican, *April 7, 1928. Holy Faith is the Episcopal Church shown near the center of the map. The numbers represent properties for sale. Nos. 36 and 148 are houses priced at $4000 and $3800 respectively; No. 148 is a lot for sale at $23 as front foot.*

Cutting, the newspaperman and politician whom we have already met, was junior warden through Trowbridge's years. Vestrymen were generally re-elected from year to year. The most prominent of them were Robert L. Ormsbee, cashier of the Capital City Bank, Julius H. Gerdes, H. H. Dorman, William J. Barker, Frank P. Newhall, the former organ blower Alfred C. Wiley, Milo G. Pray, and Dr. Harry Mera. A brother of Dr. Frank Mera who ran the Sunmount Sanitorium, Harry was an anthropologist and county health officer; it was he who sug-

49

gested the Zia sun symbol as the New Mexico state flag.[4] Most of the earlier leaders were gone. Rufus J. Palen had died in 1916, and Bradford Prince followed him in 1922.

Both the congregation and the parish budget grew modestly. In 1918 the annual parochial report sent to the bishop recorded that the church's membership was 165, with 127 communicants. A decade later the figures were 238 and 171. Trowbridge's last report, for the year 1935, lists 300 baptized members and 220 communicants. In 1932 the rector drew up, perhaps for use in his comments at the annual parish meeting, a table of baptisms, confirmations, marriages, and burials during his years in office. He had christened 193 persons, seen 163 confirmed, married 88, and buried 106, most of whom were not actually members of the parish. The figures did not change much from year to year, but Trowbridge reckoned that he had officiated at 39% of the baptisms and 44% of the weddings ever held at Holy Faith. In 1918 there had been 64 services of Holy Communion, including 52 on Sundays, and 55 offerings of Morning Prayer, 45 of them on Sundays. These had risen by 1935 to 103 Eucharists (63 on Sundays, 18 on weekdays, and 22 in the clinic) and 46 renderings of the daily offices (40 Sunday services of Morning Prayer, 6 weekday recitations of Evening Prayer).

In 1918 the parish had receipts of $3,215.06, including $1,292.00 from pledges, and expenses of $2,822.62. The rector's salary was $1200 (and was not in arrears); the organist was paid $70. Trowbridge's stipend was raised to $1500 in 1919, $2000 in 1923, $2200 in 1928, $2300 in 1930. The organist's salary had risen to $200 by 1921, when the janitor was paid $210.

This was also a time of stability and modest growth for parish organizations. There were two groups for women, the Guild and the Auxiliary. Fund raising was the most important activity of the Guild. At the beginning of our period the sums involved were relatively modest; in 1918 the treasurer, Anna D. Mardorf (the wife of C. G. Mardorf, vice-president of the Capital City Bank), reported income of $422, of which $127 had come from the annual chicken-pie dinner and sale. This was already fixed immovably on the first Friday in December; an early member, Vivvia Thornton, once suggested moving the bazaar and dinner to another date in order to avoid conflict with an event at the Woman's Club, but according to Beatrice Chauvenet "her suggestion met with such scornful, indignant response that it was a long time before she ever opened her mouth again at

---

[4] Mera was paid $25 for winning a competition sponsored by the D.A.R;. his design was later approved by the state legislature.

a Guild meeting."[5] Disbursements included $27 for a French orphan whom the Guild had adopted, $60 for the choir leader, and a $125 loan to the vestry. The Guild also paid for Easter decorations and the Christmas "greening" of the church, heating in the winter, the rectory telephone, and insurance on the organ. There were 19 meetings with an average attendance of 12. In 1922 the Guild paid $39.33 for choir vestments and $1.13 for robes for the children's choir. By 1925 the number of members had risen to 57 with an average attendance of 17. Total receipts were now $1016, of which $456 came from the Christmas sale. In 1928 earnings, mainly from the sale, were $1527, which rose to $1694 in 1929. This was the highest reported; the proceeds were $919 in 1932 and $960 in 1933. The activities recorded in 1928 were typical: in January dinner was served at the annual parish meeting; in February there was a silver tea and sale of items remaining from the bazaar; in April the Guild decorated for Easter, served an Easter breakfast, and undertook to have a lawn planted adjoining the church. May saw special decorations for Mother's Day and a Spanish supper. There was a card party in September. The most important event, of course, was the December sale and dinner. The average attendance that year was 21, with 10 new members. In 1932 68 attended the January dinner and 74 the Easter breakfast.

A substantial portion of the parish's expenses was borne by the Guild. We have noted the loan of $125 to the vestry in 1918. Regular payments were made from 1925 on; there was a gift of $500 in that year. By 1929 the amount passed on to the vestry had risen to $860. Just over $1000 was given in 1932 and $742 in 1933. This was broken down into a pledge of $420, an interest payment of $144, and a further gift of $178.

The Women's Auxiliary had a different membership, although there must have been some overlapping. There were separate meetings: in 1929 it was agreed that the Guild would meet the first Friday of each month, the Auxiliary on the third. In 1918 several gatherings had been cancelled because of the flu epidemic. Attendance, when recorded, was generally somewhat less that at Guild gatherings. Auxiliary programs dealt with serious topics, mainly missionary activities. We are told that in 1927 "after an interesting talk on China by Mrs. Palen, a special collection was taken for the rice fund of the children of China." Apparently this amounted to $151.20. Earlier, in 1921, $30 had been sent to a medical missionary in China and there were small gifts to St. Luke's Hospital, San Juan Mission, and a medical mission in Mexico. Near East relief received $65.75 in 1922. Four years later $15 was sent to Alaskan missions; $5 was contributed for

---

[5] Beatrice Chauvenet, *Holy Faith in Santa Fe* (Santa Fe, 1977), pp. 42-43.

(19) Rev. Walter S. Trowbridge, photograph from Church of the Holy Faith.

(20) Rt. Rev. Frederick B. Howden, courtesy Institute of Historical Survey.

blankets in Liberia, and gingham dresses and bloomers were sent to orphans there. African missions were the topic of study in 1929 and funds were sent to the Cuttington School in Liberia as well as to missions in Honolulu, Tokyo, and the mountains of Virginia. In 1931 the Auxiliary had meetings on Wednesdays in Lent to study India, and $12 was sent to the Church Army there, "as our Church has, as yet, no work in that country."

Other subjects were also addressed. What was perhaps the most interesting discussion was held in 1921: "on Sept. 16th the Auxiliary members took action upon the three points mentioned in Mrs. Doepps' letter relating to women being on equal terms with the Laymen of the Church. The three points were voted upon separately. Sec. 1 was approved by a majority of 14-7, Sec. 2 was unanimously opposed, Sec. 3 was also opposed." One wishes the secretary had told us the contents of each proposal; it was obviously too early for a feminist agenda to find favor. At the meetings in September, October, and November 1930 the Auxiliary "studied our Prayer Book, its history and the revised book we are now using"–the Guild had raised funds to pay for acquiring copies of the new 1928 Book of Common Prayer and additional Hymnals. In February 1930 there had been a talk on heresies and church councils, completing a Lenten study of the early church. Their leader and "faithful president" was Helen Chauncey Bronson Hyde, wife of Benjamin T. B. Hyde, the explorer of Pueblo Bonita at Chaco Canyon and "Uncle Bennie" to hundreds of Boy Scouts. It was Mrs. Hyde who gave the land which now forms Hyde State Park to New Mexico in memory of her husband.

Auxiliary members already used Blue Boxes to collect money for the United Thank Offering. The amount given increased steadily: $38 in 1920, $42 in 1922, $65 in 1925, $80 in 1926, $106 in 1928, and $142 in 1929. In 1931 73 women used Blue Boxes and contributed a total of $448, the largest sum given so far.

Father Trowbridge himself served as superintendent of the Sunday School, and his second wife, Jessie Carroll, was its treasurer for many years. In fact she was active in the Sunday School even before their marriage. At the beginning there were 35 students and 7 teachers, only one of whom was a man. By 1924 there were 51 students and 9 teachers; in that year $2.53 was spent to purchase anthem books for the boys' choir. The next year the school sent a Christmas box worth $13.50 to the Indian School at the Cheyenne Agency. There were six classes in 1927, with an average attendance of 38. "The Christmas entertainment, under the direction of Mrs. Parker and Mrs. Trowbridge, consisted of a one act playlet by the Primary department and a Christmas pageant by the older children. The entertainment was well put on and very much enjoyed by the parents and friends attending. This year the children brought special contributions and a Christmas box was sent to a mission school in North Carolina. In this box were eleven ties and eleven sets of checkers and checker boards for the boys, and 14 handkerchiefs and 14 strings of beads for the girls."

By 1928 enrollment had risen to 65, with an average attendance of 46. In addition to the Christmas pageant there was a "delightful" June picnic in the Tesuque valley and a "jolly" Hallowe'en party at the church. These entertainments continued for a number of years. In 1930 the senior warden, Charles Barker, took over a class of boys, and the rector also taught a group of young men. A violin solo by Mrs. E. B. Godfrey graced the Christmas pageant, and a beautiful creche was given to the school by Mrs. Hyde. In 1931 the church school helped purchase a motion picture machine which, together with a screen and a bulb, cost $203–it was being paid for over time, at $10 a month. Motion pictures were frequently shown for the Sunday School , and on one occasion the rector had members of the Auxiliary view a film demonstrating the correct use of vestments and hangings. The custom of giving each Church School student a small growing plant at Easter began about 1930 and "much pleased" the children. At the end of Trowbridge's ministry the Sunday school reported 105 students, 11 teachers, and an average attendance of 81.

A Girls' Friendly Society was active in 1918; it had 15 members and contributed $32 for a new bathtub in the rectory as well as $4 for varnishing the kneeling benches in the church. But by 1920 it was reported to be "quiescent," and it remained so for a number of years. A Church Periodicals Club was organized in May 1920. Originally its members contributed copies of nineteen periodicals which were sent to such places as "Virginia on the east, Mississippi and New Mexico on the south, Montana on the north, and west as far as Anking [sic], China. At Christmas fifty Christmas cards were sent to Miss Peters' Indian mission [together with] a small collection of paper covered books regarding famous men, especially for boys." Thirty-four magazines were regularly contributed in 1922, when $10 was sent to the library of St. Paul's College in Tokyo. The club did not make regular reports, or if it did they have not survived, but it was still operating in 1933 when five persons passed on copies of 22 magazines. In addition Mrs. Trowbridge, the indefatigable secretary, noted that "250 books were given to the Library, Laboratory of Anthropology, and individuals in rural districts."

A final group was, of course, the Altar Guild. It was always fairly small, with 10 members in 1918, 15 in 1920, and 14 in 1930, when Doris Barker, wife of the senior warden, was secretary-treasurer. In 1934 Mrs. Hyde organized her Sunday School class into a Junior Altar Guild whose 15 members helped clean and dust the church once a month. The Altar Guild budget was never large; expenses included $6.50 for cleaning hangings (1919), $55 for candlesticks (1922), and $30.25 for copies of the new Prayer Book (1929). The most expensive purchases were a new green chasuble, maniple, stole, and burse and veil ($35.02) and a white burse and veil ($33) in 1932. Green altar hangings costing $87 were added in 1933, and a green dossal and black silk hangings for the altar and pulpit followed in 1934. The rector built a new cabinet in which they were stored, and the old white and green hangings were sent to a mission at Hot Springs, Arkansas. Expenses for flowers ran about $20 a year; following services the arrangements were taken to parishioners who were ill.

One of Bishop Howden's dreams was the establishment of a boarding school for girls in Santa Fe. In 1920 he brought a property east of the church, extending through to Hillside Avenue, for this purpose. In 1921 there were 56 students who paid a total of $2284 in tuition, the rector himself serving as the principal, but boarders were never accommodated and the school closed in 1927. One of the women interviewed by Beatrice Chauvenet, Virginia Bliss, remembered that "like all the other girls, I was required to wear a hat and gloves to school. Tea was served every day, and we were taught to be proper ladies."[6]

✝

The most important event of these years was the construction of a parish house. A special meeting of the congregation was held May 3, 1922, to discuss the feasibility of undertaking such an ambitious project. Sixteen members were present. Minutes written by Reese P. Fullerton, acting secretary, give a succinct account of the proceedings.

> [There were] extended remarks by Rev. Walter S. Trowbridge, the rector, as follows: That the meeting in effect was more a conference than a parish meeting; that the purpose of the meeting was to ascertain if we desired to go ahead with plans for a parish house, and an outline of the proposition was presented; suggested the possible sale of the present schoolhouse and lot at perhaps a figure of $2500; that

[6] Chauvenet, pp. 43-44.

another source of revenue was, of course, the sale of the Bolander house [a property which had recently been acquired by the church] which was sold for about $2700 but of which total there would be only about $2000 on account of a necessary refund of some $700 for moneys expended for back taxes, repairs, sewer fund, etc.; that he had in mind a building say about 40 x 80 or a little larger to be erected East of the church building about on the present fence line, and fronting on a line with the front of the church; it was suggested that we should put in at least $1000 on the lot; that it might be possible to borrow money from the Church Building Fund Commission at probably a very low rate of interest, if we needed to, but would not care to consider that now; considered it best to have the said parish building act for two purposes, namely, to house the parish school and also take care of all social activities of the church; that we might as a beginning put up the building only part way—a basement and one story with temporary roof; that it probably would not be advisable to burden ourselves too heavily with debt all at once.

After Charles Barker had given some details of the Bolander house transaction there ensued "a general discussion as to the kind of building, whereabouts on the lot it might be best to place it, whether we should or should not have a half basement, etc." Finally the rector "put the question as to whether we as a parish meeting would like to have the Vestry invest $1000 in the lot, that is to take $1000 from the Bolander money and pay it on the said lot . . . where we are contemplating erecting the parish house, the Vestry not wishing to take the action without the approval of the parish. It was the consensus of opinion that the Vestry should do so." After the rector named a building committee composed of the two wardens together with the presidents, secretaries, and treasurers of the Guild, the Auxiliary, and the Altar Guild the meeting adjourned at 9:20 p.m.

The architect chosen to design the parish house was John Gaw Meem. Although he was not the originator of the so-called Santa Fe style—that honor belongs more properly to Isaac Hamilton Rapp, who also had Holy Faith connections—Meem is rightly honored as its chief advocate and practitioner.[7] The

---

[7] I am grateful to Nancy Meem Wirth for discussing her father's career with me. The chief studies of Meem and his work are Bainbridge Bunting, *John Gaw Meem, Southwestern Architect* (Albuquerque, 1983), Beatrice Chauvenet, *John Gaw Meem, Pioneer in Historic Preservation* (Santa Fe, 1985), and Chris Wilson, *Facing Southwest: The Life and Houses of John Gaw Meem* (New York, 2001). None of these say much about Meem's work at Holy Faith. On Rapp

*(21) Mr. and Mrs. John Gaw Meem and daugher Nancy, photo by Tyler
Dingee, courtesy Museum of New Mexico, Neg. No. 20719.*

story of his life is well known. He was the fourth to bear his unusual name; a long line of Meem men attended the Virginia Military Institute and worked as architects or engineers. Meem's grandfather helped design the first railroad in Brazil before serving as a colonel in the Confederate army. His father also specialized in engineering but then entered the ministry of the Episcopal church and went to Brazil as a missionary in 1891, founding a new congregation at the coastal town of Pelotas. It was here that John Gaw Meem IV was born in 1894. When he was not quite sixteen he sailed to the United States to enroll at VMI. He served as a captain in the U.S. Army during World War I, helping to train recruits in Iowa, but shortly after its end he became one of the victims of the dread influenza epidemic. In his case the illness turned into tuberculosis. In later years he recalled walking despondently down Fifth Avenue in New York City until he saw a poster promoting the Southwest in the window of a Santa Fe railway office. His doctor had mentioned the possibility of recuperating in the desert climate, so he bought a ticket to New Mexico. He arrived in Santa Fe in 1920, began treatment at Dr. Frank Mera's Sunmount Sanitorium, and soon became friends of such Santa Fe luminaries as Mary Austin, Witter Bynner, Edgar Lee Hewett, Sylvanus G. Morley, Frank Applegate, Will Shuster, and Alice Corbin and her husband William Penhallow Henderson. Perhaps his most important friendship was that with Carlos Viera, who was already designing homes in the vernacular adobe style of the Southwest.

After a year and a half at the sanitorium Meem was well enough to move to Denver, where he studied Beaux Art architecture. In 1924 he returned to Santa Fe and opened his own architectural practice in a cottage near the sanitorium made available to him by Frank Mera. His fellow Sunmount patient Cassius McCormick became his partner and served as business manager until 1928, when he returned to Chicago. Although Meem attended Holy Faith only infrequently, he found friends there, including Mrs. Rufus Palen, Mrs. Ashley Pond, and Mary Vilura Conkey. Still another of those who came to Santa Fe seeking improved health, "Lura" Conkey had been educated at St. Lawrence University and had taught Latin and Greek at a girls' school in the East. She was confirmed at Holy Faith in 1943 and served the parish devotedly for the remaining twenty years of her life.

---

see Carl D. Sheppard, *Creator of the Santa Fe Style: Isaac Hamilton Rapp* (Albuquerque, 1988). One of Rapp's buildings was a home, not in the Santa Fe style, for Bronson Cutting. It still stands at 608 Old Santa Fe Trail.

Meem was still a young man (not yet married) when he first worked for Holy Faith, and the parish house was one of his earliest buildings. Other commissions soon came his way. His addition to La Fonda, the hotel near the Plaza, dates from 1927 (the original structure had been designed by Rapp) and in 1930 he won the competition for the Laboratory of Anthropology funded by John D. Rockefeller, Jr. Once of his earliest houses was designed for Lura Conkey in 1927. At about this time Meem was also chosen as architect for a new Fine Arts Center in Colorado Springs. The principal patron of this project, Alice Bemis Taylor, introduced Meem to her niece, Faith Bemis, who had studied at Vassar and had an advanced degree from the Cambridge School of Domestic and Landscape Architecture. Faith's father was head of the family manufacturing firm in Boston but would have preferred to build homes; her mother was the daughter of a Congregational minister. Since Faith had lost her job in New York City due to the depression, Aunt Alice suggested that she assist Meem in drafting plans for the Arts Center. She soon moved to Santa Fe, where she stayed with Lura Conkey until she and John were married (in Boston) in 1933. The Meems became enthusiastic about the church in 1940 when four English evacuees fleeing the German bombing arrived to live with John, Faith, and their daughter Nancy. The young women were good Anglicans and wished to attend services at Holy Faith, and the Meems began to accompany them regularly.[8]

In building the parish house Meem worked closely with Ellen Palen, who donated $15,000 herself and agreed to help raise the remaining funds needed. One of her schemes involved the Guild. At one meeting Mrs. Palen read the parable of the talents and then gave every member a handkerchief containing 25 cents as "seed money" so that each could start her own fund for the parish house. According to Beatrice Chauvenet "Mrs. Carroll, mother of the rector's wife, had special expertise as a darner of socks. She agreed to mend all socks brought to her for five cents a pair, and this was such a bargain that some housewives brought her their holey family socks by the bushel-basketful." Another enterprising member, Vivvia Thornton, made more than $200 by selling home-made bread.[9] Records of the Talent Fund exist for several years in the '20s and early '30s. By January

---

[8] I owe this information to the Meems' daughter Nancy Wirth. The Meems always occupied the same pew at Holy Faith, near the front on the right-hand side. Following their death it was taken over by Pat and Suzanne Spivey. Unlike some other churches in both England and the United States, Holy Faith never had officially assigned seats or pew rents, which were common until the twentieth century.

[9] Chauvenet, p. 45.

1923 there was $498.20 on hand; before the end of the year more than $665 had been raised and the Guild had a certificate of deposit for $1,187.41. The cornerstone for the new building was laid by Bishop Howden in September 1925 and paid for with $60 raised by the Sunday School .

The building was completed in 1926. By this time the Guild had secured donations totaling $6143 and borrowed $17,000 from the First National Bank so that it could pay Meem and McCormick $1000 and the builder, Anthony Windsor, $15,475.24. The Guild's disbursements in 1927 included $250 more to Meem, $7408 to Windsor, $1579 to the plumber, and $1064 for parish house furnishings. As if this was not enough, the Guild fitted up a basement room in the parish house for use by the Boy Scouts in 1929, equipped the stage with curtains and a cyclorama in 1930, and had the roof painted in 1931. It is said that the architect and builder did not always see eye to eye, especially about the way in which the walls met the roof, but that Mrs. Palen (who lived just east of the construction site and kept a close eye on the work) supported Tony Windsor. Although for many years the building continued to be known as the parish house rather than Palen Hall, it was dedicated at Ellen Palen's wish to the memory of her daughter Caryl.[10]

Mrs. Palen herself died in June 1927, only a few weeks after the dedication ceremony. She had been president of the Guild for 35 years, and (having no direct heirs) she bequeathed her home to the church, together with a note for $18,000 from C. C. Catron, secured by a mortgage on his residence. The Palen house was estimated to be worth $10,000 and was rented out at $50 a month. In 1928 the parish's debt on the parish house was shifted from the First National Bank to the American Church Building Fund. This amounted to $8000 and was being paid at the rate of $800 a year. It is interesting to note that the loan was carried in the name of the Holy Faith Corporation, a body distinct from the vestry. About half of the members of the Corporation were women, including Mrs. Barker, Mrs. Wiley, Mrs. Asplund, Mrs. Ormsbee, Mrs. Harry Mera, Mrs. Kaune, and Mrs. Waltner. Other than the building committee, this was the earliest involvement of women in parish governance, and a fitting tribute to the role of the Guild.

By 1931 the Hook and Hastings organ was no longer felt to be adequate for Holy Faith—one can only wonder why—so an organ fund was established by the

---

[10] Materials relating to the construction of Palen Hall are in the Meem archives in the Southwest Research Center at Zimmerman Library, University of New Mexico, Boxes 12 and 12B.

Guild (who else?) with an initial donation of $100. On June 16 and 17 the Guild sponsored showings of the movie "June Moon" as a benefit for the organ fund. In 1932 there was a time deposit of $301.77 for the organ; this had risen to $436.77 by 1934.

Throughout these years the parish made substantial annual contributions to the Nation Wide Campaign which had been initiated by the national church. The funds were used for the work of the National Council, primarily missionary activity; the Campaign replaced an earlier national Every Member Canvas. In 1919 a total of $1451 was subscribed, the largest donors being Bronson Cutting ($600), Ashley Pond (founder of the Los Alamos School for Boys, $330), Ellen Palen ($300), the rector ($154), and Mrs. I. H. Rapp (widow of the architect, $100). Pledges for the three-year period ending in 1922 amounted to $2925. About $500 a year was sent annually between 1923 and 1931.

†

In addition to his work in Santa Fe Walter Trowbridge assisted several missions. The most important of these was St. Stephen's, Española. Like Holy Faith it had an active Woman's Guild; in 1920 the mission itself listed donations of $97.87 and the Guild reported receipts of $284.52. In 1922 the mission paid $500 for pews, plus freight and installation charges. Trowbridge's expenses of $64.50 were met, and the organist, a Mrs. Sargent, was given $9 a year. Those pledging included two men and nine women. There were only three pledges in 1925, six in 1926. Income in 1928 was $102; expenses included $45 for Trowbridge, $6 for the choir's meals at a hotel, and $4 for flowers given to the organist at Easter. Surviving reports from missions in Taos and Pecos begin in that year; these were small operations, with only two meetings held at Taos ($8 received, balance on hand 40 cents) and collections of $28 at Pecos. Pecos did spend $30 on hymnals in 1929, when Trowbridge's car expenses were $10. But the church in Española remained more successful, raising nearly $1000 in 1930 and spending $400 on plastering. In 1931 there were seven services at Holy Apostles mission in Taos; Pecos purchased a new altar and chancel rail, and Española gave $31 to charity. These missionary activities seem to have come to an end shortly thereafter. In 1933 Trowbridge told his friends in Taos that he would no longer be able to serve them, and Richard F. Oakley responded, "I am sorry that you will have to cut out your periodical visit to us but I truly realize and have often thought that your visits were not of monetary value but the few who had the pleasure of hearing you were revived in spirit to keep on going, also we know that with advancing years it was quite a hardship to make these trips up here." There had only been three services that year, with offerings of $9.85. Work at Española continued, however, in 1935.

Trowbridge also ministered to some of the people who lived in remote mountain homes. In July 1928 he was called to the upper Pecos, near Cowles, to officiate at the funeral of Jim Bullock, known as the hermit of the Pecos, who had died at the age of 78. A recluse, Bullock had moved to New Mexico from Missouri before the turn of the century and put up a cabin at an area called Seven Pines. In 1898 he had joined several other men from New Mexico in searching for gold in Alaska. They were unsuccessful and soon returned to the Pecos wilderness, where Bullock built a new cabin at Carpenter Ridge and attempted to mine copper. He is supposed to have killed the last mountain sheep in the area in 1902 and to have kept a large number of cats. It is unfortunate that we do not know more about his relationship with the church or with the Rev. Mr. Trowbridge.[11]

It is sad to relate that Trowbridge's last years in Santa Fe were marred by the effects of depression in the national economy and division within the parish. The stock market crash of 1929 was finally being felt. As Bishop James Stoney wrote, "The year 1931 was a difficult one everywhere in the nation. It was a time of unemployment, of bankruptcies and of bank failures. Local budgets were cut to the bone in many places. The National Council was just as deeply in distress and had to trim many budgets and withdraw some commitments." The diocesan budget fell to a bottom of $48,000 in 1933.[12] At Holy Faith, gifts to the Nation Wide Campaign in 1932 were $100 short of the quota for the first time. At their February meeting members of the Auxiliary discussed the financial crisis of the church. In December 1935 the parish treasurer, Mr. Ormsbee, reported that the rector's salary was $275 in arrears for 1933, $650 for 1934, and $500 for 1935. There were unpaid bills totaling $4,202.14 with only $30.05 cash on hand, and $1920 was still owed on the parish house note. Even the Guild had overspent its income by about $700.

An anonymous short history in the parish archives attributes Father Trowbridge's departure to ill health, and the letter from Taos certainly suggests that he was finding it difficult to manage all his activities. But there was more to it than that. Writing about twenty years after the event, Beatrice Chauvenet remembered the true situation.

[11] Merideth A. Hmura, *Mountain View Ranch: 1915-1945* (Lockport, Ill.: Leaning Pine Publishing Co., 1996), pp. 48-49.
[12] Stoney, pp. 132, 137.

Sadly, as too often happens, the rector became the center of dissension as contentious groups sought to dominate policies and practices. There were some who favored "low church" services, with a minimum of ritualistic ceremony and others who enjoyed the "high church" more elaborate ritualism. In 1935, after his eighteen years of devoted service to the parish, Mr. Trowbridge was asked to resign by the Vestry. It was only two years until he would be eligible for full retirement, and he had expected to complete this twenty-year period in Santa Fe. Walter and Jessie Trowbridge loved Holy Faith and Santa Fe; it was with some bitterness that they left the parish and accepted a transfer to Oklahoma.[13]

Some must have thought Trowbridge too high church. As we have seen, he began wearing eucharistic vestments, including a maniple (this is a ceremonial towel worn around the priest's wrist) as well as a chasuble. The annual lists of services also suggest that Holy Communion was being celebrated more often (always once a Sunday, and sometimes twice) while Morning Prayer was being said less frequently. The church's movement towards making the Eucharist the principal service each Sunday was beginning, after centuries when a monthly or quarterly Communion was the general practice, and many who had grown to love Morning Prayer regretted the change. It may be, too, that there was some unhappiness with the new Book of Common Prayer. Today some conservatives still prefer the 1928 services and may be surprised to learn that they were not uniformly welcomed at the time. Those who had opposed their introduction included Santa Fe's own Bradford Prince. Shortly before his death Prince had written a treatise deploring liturgical change and arguing that there was no need to alter existing services. This was printed in *The Churchman*.[14] The rector may have been unpopular with some because of his adherence to the officially sanctioned liturgy.

Walter S. Trowbridge resigned on October 25, 1935, and left for Miami, Oklahoma, a month later. The mellowing years had come to an end.

---

[13] Chauvenet, p. 47.
[14] Chauvenet, p. 63.

5. Kinsolving as Rector, 1936-1953

The Rev. Charles James Kinsolving, III, served Holy Faith as rector from 1936 to 1953. His family included a number of leading churchmen. Although he had been born in Brooklyn, Kinsolving spent most of his early life in Texas; he was educated at the Terrill Preparatory School in Dallas and then at the Massachusetts Institute of Technology and the University of the South at Sewanee. All of his degrees were from Sewanee: B.A. 1925, B.D. 1930, and D.D. 1954. He was ordained to the priesthood by Bishop Moore of Dallas in January 1929. After a brief term as curate at St. Matthew's Cathedral in Dallas he moved to Denton; he was priest-in-charge there and in Commerce, Texas. In 1932 he married Mary Virginia Robinson. The couple had two sons, Charles James IV and John.[1] As Beatrice Chauvenet commented, the young family that occupied the rectory for the next sixteen years soon captured the affection of parishioners.[2]

The parish grew substantially during Kinsolving's years. Annual reports track the increases in the number of baptized persons and communicants.[3] In 1936 the congregation counted 358 baptized members and 280 communicants. By 1940 the figures had grown to 463 and 322 respectively. The next year the rector was disappointed to note "that for the second consecutive year the Parish shows no growth. The explanation of that fact is to be found not only in the large number of people removing from Santa Fe in recent months,[4] but also in the fact that it

---

[1] Biographical information from James M. Stoney, *Lighting the Candle: The Episcopal Church on the Upper Rio Grande* (Santa Fe, 1961), p. 221.

[2] Beatrice Chauvenet, *Holy Faith in Santa Fe* (Santa Fe, 1977), p. 49.

[3] Unless otherwise noted all information in this chapter is taken from files of annual reports in the parish archives, Boxes I.2 and I.3.

[4] Helen Hyde, corresponding secretary of the Guild, noted that during the year

(22) Rt. Rev. Charles J. Kinsolving III, photo courtesy Institute of Historical Survey.

(23) Rt. Rev. James M. Stoney, photo courtesy Institute of Historical Survey.

has been impossible to plan ahead for confirmations due to the existing vacancy in the Episcopate of the District"–Bishop Howden had died in November 1940 and was not succeeded by Bishop Stoney until 1942.[5] But by 1945 the congregation had grown to 560 (this included 150 families and 86 individual members), with 416 communicants. The figures for 1948 were 724 members (180 families plus 115 individuals) and 508 communicants. The rector was then able to include positive comments in his report to the annual meeting, given the title "Parish Progress."

> While it is not of any particular importance, figures in the growth of membership in a Church such as 500, 1,000, and 2,000 seem to possess a significance of their own. Up until the year 1948 we have been on the way to achieving a communicant strength of 500. Now we are no longer on our way to 500, we are on our way to 1,000. As of December 31, 1948, there were 508 communicants in this Parish. We have reached and passed an objective. Now a new objective is ours–another round number of no real worth in itself, 1,000.

> How long will it take us to attain this new objective? Five years? A decade? A quarter of a century? To some extent, of course, it depends upon the growth of Santa Fe. To a much greater extent it depends upon the missionary spirit and enthusiasm for the Church of the Holy Faith, of the Episcopal Church. We can eventually reach this figure of 1,000 if Santa Fe grows to a town of 50,000.

Kinsolving was not to see his new goal reached. When he left in 1953 the parish had 682 communicants. Santa Fe did not grow to be a town of 50,000 until the early 1980s; the population was 49,299 in 1980 and 55,859 in 1990.[6]

The size of the parish budget also increased steadily. When Kinsolving assumed office the annual revenue was $7277, of which $2240 came from pledges. By 1939 it was $8415, pledges accounting for $3039. Funds borrowed for a building program artificially inflated income for the next two years; in 1942 revenues were

---

she had sent four letters of appreciation and regret to members who had moved away.

[5] Frederick B. Bartlett, bishop of the missionary district of Idaho, had been given responsibility for overseeing work in New Mexico at the time of Howden's death but he did not come to the state and died in an automobile accident in December 1941. See Stoney, p. 220.

[6] Figures from Henry J. Tobias and Charles E. Woodhouse, *Santa Fe: A Modern History, 1880-1990* (Albuquerque, 2001), p. 214.

$8517 with pledges of $3717. In 1945 pledges and donations accounted for $6442 of a total budget of $10,067. The year 1948 saw a budget of $15,560; 1950 had revenues of $22,198, and 1952 income of $25,764. This was more than three times what it had been in 1936. The rector's salary, $1333 in 1936, was increased to $2000 in 1937 and $2400 in 1938. It remained at that level until 1943, when it went up $200. Another $200 was added in 1944. By 1946 the stipend was $3600, then $4200 in 1948 and $5100 in 1952, Kinsolving's last full year. After 1945 he also enjoyed a car allowance, originally $120 but rising to $240 and then $360. The parish also made significant contributions to his retirement fund and, of course, provided a rectory. In addition to meeting these local expenses Holy Faith continued to support the Nation Wide program of the national church. Contributions, raised separately from the parish budget, amounted to $379 in 1936 and $467 in 1937, when the Church School sent its Easter offering of $135 and the largest donor, Helen Hyde, gave $50. In 1940 the parish gave $651, exceeding its quota of $574. By 1945 the missionary quota (paid to the diocese rather than the national church and no longer called Nation Wide) amounted to $1017 and was paid out of the regular parish budget. Holy Faith's contributions to the diocesan budget generally ranked third, just below those of St. Clement's in El Paso and St. John's in Albuquerque.

During the 1930s and 1940s parish leaders continued to serve long terms. R. L. Ormsbee remained as treasurer from 1936 until 1945; in 1940 he also served as senior warden. Others who served as wardens include John W. Chapman, Henry Dendahl, Dr. A. S. Lathrop, E. R. Wood, and Henry E. Kaune. Later treasurers included James C. Scott and Harvey Thiele. Vestrymen always had three-year terms and were often re-elected; among them one finds the names of A. C. Wiley, Reginald Fisher, W. E. Strohm, and John Gaw Meem. A resolution presented by the vestry to the annual meeting in 1947 said "that Vestrymen whose terms expire at the time of any given Annual Parish Meeting are ineligible for election to the Vestry until the time of the next Annual Parish Meeting." This was passed, and it did have the effect of ensuring more frequent turn-over of parish officers.

Parish organizations experienced ups and downs, although in general they grew as well. In 1936 the Church School had eleven teachers (three of them male) and 122 students (44 boys and 78 girls). The number of pupils had fallen to 105 in 1940, but there were 135 in 1945, despite an epidemic of flu and colds which reduced attendance, and 150 in 1947. Rather surprisingly the number of boys (85) exceeded girls (65)—this was to be common for the next decade—although as usual more women than men served as teachers (there were four men in a staff of eighteen). The 1940 report includes the comment that more teachers were needed, for no class should be larger than twenty. In 1941 there were ten classes serving 34 children in the primary division, 53 in intermediate grades, and 33 in junior and senior high school–"the number of children in the primary department has increased so much that it was necessary to buy another long table and twelve little chairs in the autumn," the secretary said. Steady growth was noted in the report for 1949, when there were 175 students. By 1950 the number of students had reached 196 and there was talk of dividing the school into two sections, coordinated with both the 9:30 and 11:00 services, or perhaps opening a new group to meet at Kaune School. This was not done, but by the time of Kinsolving's departure the number of pupils exceeded 200.

Opening services for the primary department were held in the Holy Innocents chapel which had been fitted up in the balcony of Palen Hall. Older children attended the 9:30 family service in the church, music for which was provided by the Junior Choir. The liturgy was Morning Prayer on three Sundays with Holy Communion once a month–the most common arrangement in churches throughout the country during these years.[7] Sunday School offerings were sufficient to pay for materials and supplies; a Lenten offering was always given to work outside the parish, and special gifts were frequently sent to aid in missionary efforts throughout the world. There were also special activities, generally the same each year: the Christmas pageant, at which the Junior Choir sang; a summer picnic; the Hallowe'en party; and a Thanksgiving service, again with music by the Junior Choir. In 1945 there were 35 boys and girls in the Junior Choir, and Gertrude Clark was named as co-director with the organist, Grace Robinson Fisher, "because the large number of children in the choir could not be handled by one person." These leaders complained in 1946 that greater parental cooperation was needed, as there were often 25 at a service but only 6 or 8 at the rehearsal which preceded it. Later the rule that only those who had attended the rehearsal might sing the service was firmly enforced. Senior members of the choir (those in high school) had to memorize the canticles, parts of the communion service, and a number of hymns. For several years at about this time the choir sang for Church School gatherings held on Friday afternoons during Lent. In

---

[7] In the 1960s the author of this history was organist and choirmaster of the Church of the Good Shepherd in Austin, Texas, where his Junior Choir of about thirty members sang for a 9:30 family service with a monthly Communion and Morning Prayer on other Sundays, just as at Holy Faith.

1950 there was a waiting list of about a dozen boys and girls who wished to join but could not be accommodated immediately. Services for young children were held throughout the year, but classes for older boys and girls generally did not meet during the summer months, and choir attendance was down.

†

Throughout these years the Holy Faith Guild remained active and continued to raise substantial sums of money, still primarily from the Christmas bazaar and sale. In 1936 the total income had been $1269, with $928 coming from Guild earnings. By 1939 earnings provided $1377 (the highest sum so far) of revenues totaling $2436. These figures fell somewhat during the earlier years of World War II, but in 1943 income was $2252 with earnings accounting for $773. Guild revenues were $2138 in 1946, $2614 in 1949, and $2331 in 1953. A fixed sum of $420 was given to the vestry each year for parish expenses. Contributions to the United Thank Offering rose from $108 in 1939 to $399 in 1953, the highest sum being $441 in 1949. Annual gifts were also made to missions, the sums ranging from a low of $103 in 1940 to a high of $281 in 1943. In addition the Guild began making contributions to charitable activities within Santa Fe, a typical grant being about $200. Membership was usually said to be about 40, with an average attendance of 15 or 16 at the monthly meetings. Mrs. Harry Mera continued to serve as treasurer for many years before retiring in 1944.

Mary Kinsolving, the rector's wife, was recording secretary in 1941 and contributed some interesting comments to the annual parish report. The year, she wrote, was very successful.

> Many interesting programs were given at the various meetings, the theme for these programs being "Forward in Service." Several guest speakers gave interesting talks, including Mrs. Tabor from the National Council. During the year three food sales were held. The garden tea was held in July at the home of Mrs. and Mrs. Henry Dendahl. In June a bridge tea was given in the parish house, and in October [there was] an Exhibition of "Things Antique and Unique." The Guild also sponsored "The Troubadors" for two performances in July. One of the outstanding accomplishments of the Guild during 1941 was the appointment of a permanent Social Service Committee and the setting aside of $10 a month for its use. This committee has functioned well throughout the year, working in conjunction with the Maternal Health Center, and has brought help,

temporary relief, and comfort to several families.[8]

In 1943, in addition to serving as organist, Grace Fisher was the Guild's recording secretary. "During the past year," she wrote, "the Guild has carried on many of its usual functions in spite of world conditions. Although the attendance has not been large, those who have come have been very faithful. The Guild, under the able leadership of Mrs. Clyde Parrish, served the January supper and the Easter breakfast. It was with deep regret that the Guild accepted Mrs. Parrish's resignation as president when she left town in June. Mrs. Kinsolving, elected by acclamation to fill her place, finished out the year in a most efficient manner. One particular evidence of this was the outstanding success of the bazaar this year." In September the Guild served a special supper honoring newcomers; about a hundred attended. Several of the programs given in 1945 were particularly interesting. Dr. Edgar L. Hewett, a distinguished anthropologist and director of the Museum of New Mexico, gave an illustrated lecture on his visit to the Holy Land, and a few months later Mrs. Dietrich "told of her visit to India showing treasures she had brought home."[9] The Guild sponsored a violin concert by Waldemar Geltch, a member of the faculty at the University of Kansas and a fine performer.[10] There was a parish dinner honoring Deaconess Putnam, who had retired after spending many years as a missionary in China; another "delightful parish supper" featured music and a motion picture. Like other parishioners, members of the Guild were saddened to hear of the death of Bishop Howden's son, chaplain Frederick B. Howden, Jr., who had died in a Japanese prison camp following the famous Bataan death march. It was said that he starved because he gave his meager food allowance to other prisoners. In his memory the Guild purchased a portable tryptich reredos for use by a chaplain in the Philippines.

Despite these activities there are signs that some rethinking of the Guild's organization was needed. One proposal, not implemented so far as we know, called for the establishment of neighborhood groups as a means of increasing participation. Another said that only the executive committee would meet monthly, with the full membership gathering for programs five months a year. This ap-

---

[8] The Maternal Health Center, which opened in 1937, was originally a birth-control facility sponsored by the Margaret Sanger movement. Naturally it was opposed by the Catholic church. Its strategy soon grew to dealing with maternal problems as well. See Tobias and Woodhouse, p. 217.

[9] On Hewett see Beatrice Chauvenet, *Hewett and Friends: A Biography of Santa Fe's Vibrant Era* (Santa Fe, 1983).

[10] This writer knew Professor Geltch at K.U. a few years later but was not aware that he had Santa Fe connections.

pears to have been accepted but it too was not brought into practice. A group of "business women" is mentioned in 1938, but no more is heard of it. It became harder to find women who were willing to fill Guild offices, since some who served for many years had died or were no longer able to attend meetings. In 1947 it was decided to have three presidents a year, each holding office for four months; those named were Mrs. Augustine Haughton, Mrs. Henry Kaune, and Mrs. Edward Oakley. But in following years a single president is listed. The report for 1947 said that the Guild had served punch and cookies following the 11:00 service; "this is now, however, discontinued." In 1948 the annual garden party was abandoned for the year.

In one way or another the Guild carried on most of its usual activities. This was not true, however, of the Woman's Auxiliary. It was still meeting in 1937, when it sent $10 to Kuling School in China. But parish reports after 1940 do not mention the Auxiliary, and (as we have seen) the collection of the United Thank Offering was transferred from the Auxiliary to the Guild.

A number of new groups were organized within the parish, some lasting longer than others. Most of these included both men and women. In 1939 the rector established a committee on Christian Education, explaining that Holy Faith had been selected by the National Council as a Christian Education Cooperative Center in the missionary district of New Mexico and Southwest Texas. Dr. Reginald Fisher, assistant director of the Museum of New Mexico and husband of the organist, was named chairman and members were appointed to represent a variety of parish organizations, not merely the Church School. There were supposed to be seven meetings a year, but we hear no more about them. The committee did sponsor a dance attended by about a hundred young married people; the ubiquitous Helen Hyde, secretary of the new committee, said that it was "most successful" and that "it [was] planned to have similar parties at frequent intervals as an essential part of our parish life."

†

A social service committee appears in 1941. It was perhaps a spin-off from an earlier committee of the Guild. Its chairman, Linda Parrish, told parishioners that forty-two sacks of food had been delivered to the poor, a job had been found for an unemployed man from a needy family, and a wheelchair had been provided for a cripple. A fuller report issued in 1942 said that $174 had been spent processing shoes and mittens for Christmas boxes and also mentioned, rather breathlessly, "food and milk for a family with three small children and father out of work–Baby allergic to cow's milk–bought goat's milk–Father got work in Colo. Mines so moved there. Took Mother and baby to clinic several times. Another family with three little girls, Mother, father–took food and clothes and helped father get odd jobs until June when he went to work for W.P.A. Vegetables and fruits that weren't quite so fresh were given to us by Kaune grocery." There were fewer calls for help during the summer, when most men were working. By 1948 and 1949 the service group, as it was then called, was holding several rummage sales a year and raising as much as $2264 annually. It operated the Tiny Tot Play School, provided a nursery for young children during the 11:00 church service, and sponsored children's movies and the teen-agers' dances in Palen Hall. In 1953 the service group had 48 members and held 12 meetings. It arranged young people's gatherings twice a week, featuring instruction in art and photography as well as square dancing; sold theater and rodeo tickets as well as holding rummage sales to raise money; sponsored a concert by the Denver University choir, and helped provide costumes and refreshments for the Christmas pageant.

A Holy Faith planning board held what appears to be a unique meeting at the rectory on October 15, 1947. Its chairman, Harvey Thiele, said that the group would stress fellowship and worship, including greater use of devotions at home and grace at meals. According to its minutes "the need for improving the choir was stressed"; it was suggested that hymns and anthems should relate to sermon topics, which need not be based on the Epistles and Gospels. There should be parish dinners four times a year, as well as occasional square dances. A Young People's Fellowship established in 1948 proved more permanent. It began with 39 members, 29 in high school and 10 in college, and the stated purpose of providing fun and fellowship. Several of its members still remember how important the square dances, prayer group, and summer camp at Cloudcroft were in their lives. In addition the young people sent 100 pounds of clothing to the poor in Europe, but their service was not as great as their sponsor, Helen Musgrave, could wish. In 1950 "there were a great many new names added to the list of members" and it was "a very eventful year," although the secretary did not bother to say just what the events were. The report for 1953, also not very informative, was signed by Johnny Kinsolving, the rector's younger son. In his annual report for 1949 Father Kinsolving had expressed his desire to hire a youth worker, and in 1950 he reiterated the need to find a director of religious education and youth work "at the earliest possible moment," since the person employed in July, Miss Frances Walker, had left at the end of the year. But we hear nothing about a successor.

The Altar Guild had between twelve and twenty members, plus some who were inactive because of age or because they no longer lived in Santa Fe. Small purchases of vestments and related articles continued. In 1936 two chasubles were purchased for $80. The next year $40 was spent for a red chasuble and $85.60 for a violet frontal; the Guild's report notes that "the old red chasuble was returned to Father Trowbridge (the last of the vestments loaned to us by him). The old violet hangings were sent to St. Paul's Mission at Hot Springs, New Mexico; and Friar Willis wrote that they were used with great pleasure during Advent in their little temporary chapel." It was also necessary to extend the top of the retable to keep the flowers away from the lights. A red burse and veil were provided in 1938 and material was purchased for cushions at the communion rail. Pew cushions were added in 1939 at a cost of $54.50 and the rector was given a new surplice as an Easter gift. An amusing note tells us that "in September a new faucet was selected for the Sacristy, for which the Holy Faith Guild paid, and which the Rector installed, eliminating a bill from the plumber." In addition to seeing that the altar was properly cared for, members had a number of programs relating to liturgy and theology. In 1940 these included studies of the Oxford Movement and of the practice of confession, probably to be interpreted as a sign of the increasing influence of high church beliefs. Helping with the war effort, Guild members made two sets of altar linens to be used by army chaplains, each set containing eleven pieces. Letters asking parishioners to give flowers for the altar as memorials were sent out annually, with considerable success; the Guild had to purchase flowers only one or two Sundays if at all. They were usually given on one Sunday as a memorial to Mrs. Palen.

Helen Hyde continued her faithful service as directress of the Altar Guild throughout these years. As we have seen, she was responsible for founding a Junior Altar Guild, originally composed of members of her Sunday School class. It had about 35 members through the Kinsolving years; they met monthly to help the Altar Guild by cleaning and polishing the brasses, making palm crosses for Palm Sunday, and occasionally taking flowers to shut-ins. Some of the young women were inactive because they were away attending college or because they married and had young children. Revenues and expenses were minimal; a unique expenditure was $1.99 for a baby spoon given to Mrs. John Dendahl in 1938. In 1941 $28.92 was "on hand for Jerusalem and the Jews," the missionary program supported by the parish.

The most interesting record of the acolytes, or as they were sometimes called the Servers Guild, dates from 1945. "We are proud of growing in two years from

9 to 39 members," William E. Strohm, Jr., wrote, " but we have the problem of fitting 39 boys of different sizes into 6 red cassocks, and we should be happy if any members of the parish would like to give us one or two more." Fortunately the next year's report states that "some additional red cassocks have been purchased, so at present there are various sizes, which makes it easier for every boy who wishes, to have a chance to serve." The boys were organized into several grades depending on age. The youngest served as cross guards, carrying candles on either side of the processional cross. Then there were the acolytes proper, who might serve as crucifer. High school boys who had been confirmed were known as servers and did indeed assist in serving Communion as well as reading lessons, prayers, and the Litany. Appropriate training was provided, especially at the highest level. Young boys served as acolytes for the services held in the children's chapel; in 1945 "a beautiful polychromed cross was given to the Church School by Mrs. Musgrave, as the brass cross is too heavy for the younger acolytes to carry."

The Holy Faith chapter of the Daughters of the King, named in honor of former Bishop Howden, was organized on June 12, 1942. Mrs. Hyde was secretary-treasurer and probably provided the inspiration that held the group together; their activities were low-key and involved prayer, study, and service. Originally there were only seven members, with two probationers. In 1945, 1946, and 1947 they made layettes for the Save the Children Federation. Perhaps more importantly, they visited newcomers as well as the sick and shut-ins. Eighty such visits were reported in 1945, when the total number of services (presumably including intercessory prayers) was said to be 1273. In 1948 eleven members gathered for eleven meetings. Books studied included *Whom They Pierced* by Mervyn Stockwood, the Bishop of London, and *They Saw the Lord* by the Rev. Bonnell Spencer of the Order of the Holy Cross.

The Church Periodicals Club, as we have seen, had been recycling books and periodicals since 1920. Throughout Kinsolving's years the members functioned quietly, behind the scenes, but distributed an amazing quantity of reading materials. In 1939 fifteen donors gave nearly 1500 magazines to the Santa Fe library, the Red Cross, hospitals, rural schools, and deserving families. By 1949 the number of magazines sent off had risen to 6528. The books given away, amazingly, numbered 385. In 1953 the numbers were 8754 and 350 respectively. Recipients now included the Boy Scouts and the State Library Extension Service as well as institutions in New York, Alaska, and Liberia. Once again one encounters the name of Helen Hyde as the genius in charge of the enterprise. A parish library was not organized until 1949 but within a few months eighty-five books had been gathered, some as gifts from St. Bede's Church in New York City and St. John's in Washington, D.C. These were described as being "quite recent publications on religious life, church history and symbolism, and biographies." A library group led by Grace Guest met each Monday afternoon and saw that the library was open then, as well as after the chief Sunday service. By 1952 there were 231 books and the collection continued to grow under the direction of Marion Wasson, a bibliophile who headed the library committee for the next quarter century.

In addition to these parish organizations Holy Faith sponsored Scout troops. Girl Scout Troop I had been organized in 1931 and, after a lapse, was reorganized ten years later. Its five members attended church in uniform in October 1941. As the group grew a waiting list developed and a second troop was established in 1942. Meetings were occupied with dramatics, knitting, hikes, and studying national defense; Beatrice Chauvenet, obviously a woman of diverse talents, taught first aid in 1942. By 1945 there were three units: a Brownie troop, the original intermediate troop, and Troop 16, a senior troop. When the Woman's Guild gave the girls $5 for Christmas they used it to buy canned food to be sent to starving children in Europe. The next year the Girl Scouts sent more food as well as twenty-four Friendship Boxes for Girl Scouts in Holland. In 1948 the total number of Girl Scouts was 45.

The first group for boys was Cub Scout Pack 33, organized in 1946 with three dens and 31 registered cubs. By 1948 there were also Boy Scout and Senior Scout troops with a total membership of 100. This number had dropped to 40 in 1949, and Girl Scouting had disappeared altogether because it was impossible to find leaders. Perhaps the gap was filled to some extent by the revival of the Girls' Friendly Society, which had been inactive for some years. The Boy Scout troop still existed, and there were 50 boys in three Cub Scout dens.

In addition to his work in Santa Fe, Kinsolving also assisted with the missions in Española and Taos. These were always small enterprises. St. Stephen's, Española, had an income of only $17.41 in 1936 but paid $19 for the expenses of its services. In 1938 Kinsolving was paid a salary of $39 out of a total budget of $149; there were fifteen communicants and four services of Holy Communion, none on a Sunday. In 1939 the treasurer, Arthur H. Gallup, had to acknowledge that the diocesan quota and assessments "were not paid as funds were insufficient during this period." But, as in Santa Fe, there was a Guild which raised $44.36 "through various enterprises." In 1940 services included twenty recitations of the offices (presumably Morning Prayer) by a lay reader on Sundays but only five

Eucharists, all on weekdays. The mission paid Kinsolving $48.50 for his expenses in 1942 and gave $4.60 to Bishop Stoney, probably on the occasion of a rare episcopal visit. The mission owned a church building estimated to be worth $2000.

Fewer documents for St. James's Church in Taos survive in Santa Fe, perhaps because it was not regularly served by the rector of Holy Faith, but it appears to have been more successful than the mission at Española. It 1944 and 1945 it listed Kinsolving as rector and paid him expenses–$67.50 in 1944 and $131 in 1945. In 1944 Kinsolving made eight visits. Total receipts for 1945 were $437, of which $144 had to be paid for rent. Beginning in March 1949 Holy Faith provided services for the new scientific community at Los Alamos one afternoon and evening each week. By the end of the year the church of Trinity on the Hill had been organized and was seeking a full-time clergyman who would also assume responsibility for the Taos mission, "thus [as Kinsolving wrote] freeing Holy Faith of this obligation."

It is easy to imagine that all these activities overtaxed the church's physical facilities. The next chapter will consider the expansion of the buildings during these years.

6. John Gaw Meem and the Building Era, 1939-1953

The annual parish meeting held on February 10, 1939, considered a long-term plan to improve and expand the facilities of the church. Its points, which included the expected cost of each item, were these:

(1) The purchase of land in back of Parish House, $350-400;

(2) A new heating plant for Church and Parish House, $3000;

(3) The construction of a New Rectory, $10,000;

(4) The construction of a Church School Building, $3500-4000;

(5) The construction of a Chapel between the Church and the Parish House, $6500;

(6) The construction of a new sanctuary in the Church, $6000;

(7) Miscellaneous items of repair and renovation, $1500.

"It was proposed," according to the secretary of the meeting, R. L. Ormsbee, "that these steps be accomplished in sequence, one unit of the plan being completed before the second was undertaken. The plan was accepted by the Parish."[1]

In fact the earliest work to be put in hand involved the construction of a new sacristy and office for the rector attached to the rear of Palen Hall, perhaps on land acquired in accordance with the first point of the master plan. Henry Dendahl made a substantial contribution towards this enterprise and encouraged others to follow suit.[2] Funds raised by the end of 1940 included $1594 in gifts and a bank loan for $4900. The architect, naturally, was John Gaw Meem. He was paid

---

[1] Minutes of annual meeting for 1939, parish archives, Box I.2. Unless otherwise
   noted all information in this chapter is taken from the files of annual reports.
[2] See Beatrice Chauvenet, *Holy Faith in Santa Fe* (Santa Fe, 1977), p. 49.

$321.30 for drawing plans and the contractor was paid $4573 for the construction. Some other work was undertaken at the same time. The report of the Altar Guild written by its directress, Helen Chauncy Bronson Hyde, records that "Directly after Easter the Altar was cut down and the platform around the footpace removed. Consequently the four frontals had to be shortened and the four dossals lengthened. [Then] a new Altar of different dimensions was placed in the Church. Therefore new linens have been made. The frontals have been enlarged to fit the new Altar, and the cabinet in the sacristy extended to hold the larger hangings." New Eucharistic vestments, called a Low Mass set, were given as a memorial to Mr. Hyde (the directress's late husband) and were used for the first time on Christmas Eve. According to the annual report of the Church School (also written by Mrs. Hyde) "every available spot in the Parish House, as well as the Church, was used for classes, but the conditions were so crowded that it seemed desirable to build a new rectory and use the old one for class rooms for the older pupils. However, the Parish decided that this was inadvisable at the present time."

Further repairs and improvements made in 1941 cost $2590. In 1943 moveable curtains were provided for use in the parish house in order to divide the space for use by different classes. In 1943 a gift of $770 (probably from Helen Hyde) in memory of Bishop Howden was designated for the addition of a reredos to stand above the church's new altar. An impressive work which still dominates the interior of Holy Faith, it had been designed (at Mrs. Hyde's suggestion) by Wilfred Edwards Anthony of New York City but was actually carved by one of Santa Fe's leading craftsmen, Gustave Baumann, who is best known for his multicolor woodcuts.[3] Among small contributions to the reredos fund were $50 from the Church School and $20 from the Junior Altar Guild. The total cost was about $1000. The principal figure in the reredos is Christ the King; he is flanked by St. Paul and St. John, with rays symbolizing the Light of the World flowing through them. Movable side panels which can be closed on solemn occasions such as Good Friday depict Christ's message being received by the several human races—white, black, American Indian, and Asian—flanked by a group of worshiping angels. Bishop James M. Stoney dedicated the reredos on August 12, 1945.[4]

---

[3] Baumann had joined with the writer and artist Will Shuster in fabricating the first Zozobra for the Santa Fe fiesta in 1926. See Chris Wilson, *The Myth of Santa Fe* (Albuquerque, 1997), p. 213.

[4] An illustrated pamphlet was issued at the time of the dedication of the reredos; there are a number of copies in the parish archives. Small models of portions of the Reredos are installed in the parish library.

(24) Reredos designed by Wilfred Edwards Anthony and carved by Gustave Baumann, shown in original position with Good Shepherd window above, photo from parish archives, Box II.16.

The parish house was enlarged again, much more significantly than before, in 1948. New spaces provided needed room for parish offices and Church School classes. C. J. Kinsolving's rector's report for 1948–the same one in which he commented that the number of communicants had passed 500–said that "the outstanding achievement of the year, of course, was the construction of the Parish House last summer. We have planned and worked long and hard for this. The immediate upsurge in the Church School, both in enrollment and attendance, [and] the renewed vision and enthusiasm that has come to the Parish through its sense of achievement has indicated its worth. Sacristy, class-room space and Parish offices, these have been our great needs for some years." A building fund totaling $46,269 had been raised–it included $11,984 from pledges, $925 given by several commercial firms, and $23,000 borrowed from the bank. The contractors, the Modern Construction Company, were paid $42,712, and Meem's architectural firm received a fee of $1083. The rector's report for 1949 noted that attendance at all services had increased 15%. This was no mean achievement and was due, at least in part, to better facilities. The debt had been reduced by $5000 and was then under $15,000.

But there were still problems, the worst of which involved the kitchen. It was originally located in the basement under Palen Hall. Beatrice Chauvenet's history of the parish has an amusing account of one incident, based on reminiscences by Vivvia Thornton.

> [It was] the custom [to serve] Easter Breakfast in Palen Hall between the early service and the big Easter Sunday celebration. To take care of their needs the women supplemented the three-burner oil stove in the basement with electric waffle irons. One Easter morning, as they prepared to serve, the plugging-in of the waffle irons blew the fuses in the building. The menu was hastily changed from waffles to pancakes, as they baked the waffle batter on griddles heated over the oil stove. Running up and down they congratulated one another that they had met one more emergency. However, when it came time for the eleven o'clock service it was discovered that the blown fuses rendered the electric-powered organ useless. The choir, which had been practicing special festival music for weeks, was obliged to process into the church singing *a cappella*, and the more ambitious anthems were scratched. Frustrated, Mrs. Van Stone sat at the organ, awaiting repairs by the hastily summoned electrician. She forgot that she had left the switch turned to ON, until, in the midst of the sermon, the power came back with a roar that startled and then convulsed the crowd of worshipers.[5]

The kitchen was temporarily moved to an inadequate space adjacent to the auditorium on the first floor, and finally in 1950 a proper kitchen was constructed on the east side of Palen Hall, extending almost to the street on Faithway. This addition was a project of the Guild, not the vestry. In May, Guild minutes relate, the kitchen planning committee had made its report. "In June we had a very lively busy meeting. Mr. Meem was there to show us the plans he had drawn for the kitchen. Final plans and arrangements were made for financing same. We voted to pay $20 per month on the kitchen, in addition to the original $1000, payments to start in August." The final cost was about $4850.

In June 1952 the parish was able to purchase the Payne house on Bishop's Lodge Road for use as a new rectory. "In September," according to the rector's annual report, "the old rectory, remodeled and redecorated by the vestry and refurnished by the Service Group and Library Committee, was turned over to the parish for its use. This building is now known as 'Faith House,' and is in almost daily use by numerous parish organizations and church groups." Designed

---

[5] Chauvenet, p. 50.

CRANCEL ADDITION to TRE CRVRCR OFTRE ROLY FAITR santa fe r. m

(25) Chancel addition, Church of the Holy Faith, drawing from the office of John Gaw Meem, courtesy Center for Southwest Research, University of New Mexico, No. 001-675/012-004M.

by John Gaw Meem in 1939, it provided space for seven classrooms as well as the attractive new library.[6] The new rectory, as Kinsolving said, "is a home in which the entire parish may take pride. We are most comfortable in it." Paved parking for fifty cars was provided in the area between the church and Faith House—an obvious convenience, though some lamented the loss of the former rectory garden.

The last expansion of this period involved the addition of a new chancel to the original church building.[7] Designed by Meem, this is a perfect complement to the original building and some visitors find it hard to believe that it was not part of the original scheme. Its east end (liturgically east if geographically north)

---

[6] Specifications are in the Meem archives, Southwest Research Center, University of New Mexico, File 12:26. There is also a large floor plan of the original design.

[7] Some bills and correspondence between Meem, the builder, and the rector survive in the parish archives.

(26) Drawing by Judson Studios for stained glass window of the Virgin Mary and Christ Child, Meem Job Files, Box 1, Fldr. 24, Center for Southwest Research, University of New Mexico.

(27) Drawing by Judson Studios for stained glass window of St. Francis, Meem Job Files, Box 1, Fldr. 24, Center for Southwest Research, University of New Mexico.

(28) Drawing by Judson Studios for St. Francis window showing conversion of an Indian by an early missionary, Meem Job Files, Box. 1, Fldr. 24, Center for Southwest Research, University of New Mexico.

provides a fine setting for the Anthony-Baumann reredos. In the original building this had been inserted in front of a large stained glass window depicting the Good Shepherd (a reference to the fact that the parish had at one time had that name) so that it stood in a cramped space and clashed in style with the Victorian glass. Meem retained this window but moved it to the Gospel side of the chancel and had three tall lancet windows made to stand above the altar. They are based on the Creed and designed with a number of small scenes in brilliant reds and blues. The windows were executed by the Judson Studios of Los Angeles; Meem had studied the work of several studios and was enthusiastic about the vivid luminosity of the Judson work. Their cost, $5000, was contributed by Meem as a memorial to his father, John Gaw Meem III. In 1965 two more new windows, also by the Judson Studios, were placed on the side wall: a memorial to Mary Vilura Conkey depicts the Madonna and Child, while a window showing St. Francis with some of the animals he so loved was given in memory of Louise Beveridge Burdick, a pioneer settler in Idaho, by her daughter, Helen Burdick Brown.[8] Organ pipes would eventually project above the heads of choir members on the Epistle side of the chancel, although an electronic instrument was still in

---

[8] Correspondence and drawings relating to these windows are in the Meem archives, Southwest Research Center, University of New Mexico, File12B-35 and folder marked "Holy Faith, Windows." Meem had asked Horace Judson to submit a revised sketch of the Virgin Mary, since Kinsolving had not been

(29) Exterior, Church of the Holy Faith and Palen Hall, 1949, photo by Tyler Dingee, courtesy Museum of New Mexico, Neg. No. 73776.

use during the 1950s. The vaulted wood ceiling, higher and more elaborate than that in the nave, is painted with designs in the same colors present in the new windows. A stone panel bearing a leaf design was placed under the organ loft. It had been carved in England of local limestone during the restoration of Lincoln cathedral in the later eighteenth century and was given to Faith Bemis's father, Albert Farwell Bemis, in 1927. John Gaw Meem thought that it was an appropriate reminder of the church's ancient English traditions.[9]

---

sure he liked her expression in the original design. During the dedication of the windows a dog wandered into the church, evidently paying its respects to St. Francis.

[9] The panel is described in a letter from Meem to Donald Campbell dated October 25, 1972, now in the parish archives. A minor problem encountered by Meem involved the interment of the ashes of Dr. Francis Proctor in the west wall of the nave, at a site marked by a simple stone inscribed "Proctor." Meem had been a member of the vestry when Proctor's wife Elizabeth, a parishioner, had requested this arrangement. "We were pleased to do as she asked," Meem wrote, "although Dr. Proctor was not an Episcopalian. If he was

Meem's original plan also called for the addition of a narthex and balcony at the entrance to the church, opposite the new chancel. The narthex would incorporate the existing tower and provide shelter for those entering the building during inclement weather, while the balcony (reached by a staircase opposite the tower) would seat an additional forty people. A new baptismal font would have been provided, symbolically adjacent to the entrance to the church. The architect probably also had in mind designing a more impressive façade. Unfortunately funds for this work were not available in the 1950s and it has never been undertaken. A floor plan drawn by Edward O. Holien of Meem's office in 1949 shows how the narthex would have been incorporated and also indicates the layout of the area behind Palen Hall housing parish offices and class rooms in what is now the choir room and the children's chapel in the present Guild Room.

According to the annual report for 1953, presented in January 1954, nearly $36,000 had been pledged to the Expansion Fund with $25,949 already received. A total of $32,039 had been paid out to the architects (Meem, Zehner, Holien and Associates) and the general contractor, Robert McKee. A. C. Wiley, treasurer of the fund, said that "the payment of the $9,803.99 still out in pledges will insure the completion of the program within the allowed indebtedness. The hope and expectation is that we will be in our new Church by Easter."

The new chancel and sanctuary were the crowning achievement of the Kinsolving years, but events were not to allow him to enjoy them long, at least not as rector of Holy Faith. In 1953 Bishop James Stoney announced that, pending his imminent retirement, he wished to have a bishop coadjutor named. His own installation in 1952 as the first bishop of the Diocese of New Mexico and Southwest Texas, no longer a missionary district, and the dedication of St. John's, Albuquerque, as the cathedral of the diocese marked the apex of his episcopal career. In many ways Father Kinsolving was a natural choice as his successor, for he had been active in diocesan as well as parochial activities for many years, serving as examining chaplain and chairman of the departments of Christian educa-

anything, he was probably a Congregationalist, but he was a dear man, a delightful person. As years passed Elizabeth became somewhat alienated from the church—she never was a great enthusiast—but once in a while she gave something. When we were designing the chancel I asked her if she would be willing to contribute the new windows and she said she would not. She did not believe in stained glass windows, considering them a waste of money. This all presents a little problem, because the old gentleman is there, and the question arises as to whether he is entitled to stay there forever. Or is that an uncharitable thought?" (Quoted in Chauvenet, p. 54.)

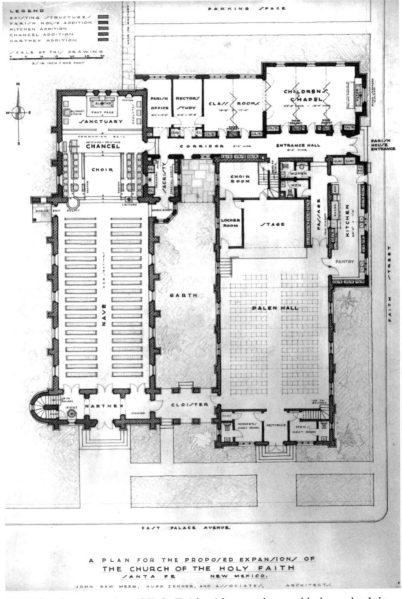

(30) Plan for expansion of Holy Faith with a narthex and balcony by John Gaw Meem office, courtesy Center for Southwest Research, University of New Mexico, No. 000-675/012-003M.

tion and social relations. On October 27, 1953, Kinsolving was consecrated bishop coadjutor, and on Stoney's retirement in 1956 Kinsolving became second bishop of the new diocese.[10] He continued to live in Santa Fe, and in 1957 John Gaw Meem designed an elegant building on Garcia Street to serve as his residence and office. In addition to providing a study for the bishop it held a chapel and room for two secretaries.[11]

After a short interim during which the Ven. L. W. Smith, diocesan archdeacon, served Holy Faith, the Rev. Henry F. Seaman succeeded Kinsolving as rector on January 1, 1954. Seaman was the son of Bishop Stoney's close friend Cecil Seaman, an Alabama native who had become bishop of North Texas. With his arrival in Santa Fe a new chapter in the history of the parish began.

[10] One may note a further way in which Kinsolving's involvement in Santa Fe society was demonstrated. He was an active member of the Chili Club, a group of twelve men organized in 1939 as the Axis Club. Its name was later changed to honor the Chili Line, the narrow-gauge railroad to Denver. This informal group enjoyed a monthly supper served in members' homes in rotation followed by a research paper written by another member. Other parishioners who belonged to the club included John Gaw Meem, the museum director Reginald Fisher, and the pediatrician Arthur Lathrop. It has been suggested that Fisher and perhaps some other members of the Chili Club were influential in putting forward Kinsolving's name as a candidate for the episcopacy. As bishop, Kinsolving still occasionally attended meetings. I am grateful to Nancy Wirth for sharing her memories of the Club. There is a history of the Chili Club written by its member the late Bill Gilbert. See also Chauvenet, pp. 51-52 (though not all of her information is accurate), and Chris Wilson, *Facing Southwest: The Life & Houses of John Gaw Meem* (New York, 2001), p. 46.

[11] Plans, specifications, and correspondence are in the Meem archives, Southwest Research Center, University of New Mexico, files 20:63 and 21:63. The building, which stood on a five acre site, was described and illustrated in the *Southwest Churchman* for September 1957. The contractor was Allen Stamm.

7. Onward, Upward, and Out, 1954-1965

In his first annual report Father Seaman described 1954 as "a wonderful year." Attendance at services had risen to 21,995—950 more than in the previous year—and giving reached a new high, $29,856, a quarter of which went for work outside the parish. The Church School was "bursting at the seams" with 258 pupils and 27 teachers. Some classes had been divided and all available room in Palen Hall and in the former rectory had been utilized, but nearly all the classes were said to be too large for effective teaching and it was suggested once again that it might be desirable to organize a second division of the school. The rector worked well with his wardens, E. R. (Ned) Wood and John Gaw Meem. The library now held 813 volumes, 277 of which were new acquisitions, and the programs of the library group included Seaman's discussion of the religious writings of C. S. Lewis. The Periodicals Club sent away 400 books and nearly a thousand magazines. The President of the Guild, Agnes Wheelwright, had "never enjoyed anything more" than her year in office, which had included a special tea to introduce the Seamans to members of the parish. Guild income of $2208 included $1315 from sales, primarily the bazaar. The 65 members of the Service Group held two rummage sales to raise money for the activities of the JEYP (Junior Episcopal Young People), mainly square dancing. The Young People's Fellowship was very active, in many cases the principal social activity for its members. It had a membership of 54 high school students who joined together for worship, dancing, and programs on such subjects as Communism and juvenile delinquency. The attendance of Junior Choir members was "much better this year," according to Pat Corelli, the director. Perhaps this was partly because choir members received tin crosses with embroidered emblems on the ribbons to honor faithful

(31) Rev. Henry F. Seaman, photo from Church of the Holy Faith.

service.[1] The acolytes enjoyed several swimming parties at La Posada. The Altar Guild purchased a new funeral pall and paid for gilding the rays of light on the reredos, funds for which had not initially been available.

The city of Santa Fe had changed greatly since the church's early years. By 1950 its population had grown to nearly twenty-eight thousand. An additional thirty-eight thousand lived in the county outside the city limits.[2] A Historical Zone Ordinance adopted in the mid-1950s mandated the preservation of the narrow streets and adobe architecture in the central area, thus assuring that the Holy Faith neighborhood would be protected even though urban sprawl might affect outlying areas. Politics were no longer dominated by the Anglos like Bradford Prince who had run both church and state during the early years; the public offices were now generally held by Hispanics, most of whom were Democrats. When the writer Tony Hillerman moved to Santa Fe in 1952 he found that "the state capital, county, and city jobs were primarily Hispanic while the Anglos were heavily into the tourism and commercial end of the game. Cultural frosting was added by a lively art colony, which was reinforced by a delegation of 'wannabe' painters, sculptors, etc., living off the largesse of wealthy kinfolks."[3] Many of the prominent Anglos still made Holy Faith their church home.

Seaman's initial congregation included just over a thousand baptized persons. The number of communicants was down from 722 to 682, but this reflected the deletion of 81 persons whose names had been removed because their domicile was unknown and 15 more who were inactive. Evidently Kinsolving had not bothered to revise his lists for several years. As Appendix 1 shows, the number of baptized members and communicants rose each year from 1954 to 1961, reaching totals of 1371 and 882 respectively. The largest number of Church School students, 342, was recorded in 1959, but there were still more than 300 in 1961. The total annual attendance at services also hit a high of 27,145 in 1959, with 26,381 in 1961, while the number of communicants (6125 in 1955–there are no statistics for 1954) did not peak until 1963, when the figure was 9269. For the remainder of the 1950s, at least, "Onward and upward" appeared to characterize the path of Holy Faith.[4]

In one of his last annual reports C. J. Kinsolving had noted that Holy Faith had grown too large to be served adequately by a single clergyman. It needed

---

[1] Nancy Meem Wirth is among those who remember receiving such crosses.
[2] Figures from Chris Wilson, *The Myth of Santa Fe* (Albuquerque, 1997), p. 330.
[3] Tony Hillerman, *Seldom Disappointed* (New York, 2001), p. 208.
[4] As usual information in this chapter is based on annual reports filed in the parish archives.

either a curate or a Director of Religious Education. Funds for such a position were provided in the budget for 1952, but (as the rector said) "due to the demand for people with specialized training in church work, it may be some time before we are successful in finding the proper person."[5] The need was finally met in 1955, when Norman F. Riebe, a "son of the parish" who had just completed his theological studies, was employed as curate. The Guild provided a luncheon in Palen Hall following his ordination in July, and the Service Group arranged a reception for him and his wife Janice at the rectory. The Riebes were active in the Church School and young people's groups but remained in Santa Fe only a year, for he received a call to be priest-in-charge of Holy Trinity Church, Raton, in 1956.[6] For the first time the parish was able to employ a full-time secretary, Miss Mary Virginia Wood, in 1955. She was also an artist, and she showed slides of the Stations of the Cross which she had created for a church in Nevada for one of the meetings of the Library Guild.

At the parish meeting in January 1956 Father Seaman said that a full-time organist and choir director was also needed and that he was then "negotiating with a well qualified and superbly trained young man to fill this position." The candidate was Joseph F. Leonard, who assumed his duties in March 1956. At the end of the year Seaman commented that "we have all rejoiced with the enrichment of our services of worship that his presence has brought. The special service of Christmas music with a twelve piece orchestra and a full choir was a beautiful climax for the year." The vestry approved larger allocations of funds for new music, new vestments were purchased, and the old kitchen was refurbished for use as a choir room. According to an anonymous report, possibly written by Mr. Leonard, the senior choir now consisted of twenty-nine women and nine men, "though it is hard to get them all at the same time." In her final report as organist and director Mrs. Fisher had said (perhaps defensively) that "It has been with the hope of nurturing congregational singing that the service music in this church has been kept simple and the same chants and communion services sung over and over again. People who sing seem to be woefully lacking in our church of 716 communicants." Mrs. John McHugh, who had been in England, brought back several new anthems including Ralph Vaughan Williams' setting of the introit

---

[5] Mrs. James D. Sears was listed as Director of Religious Education and Young in 1951 but she served less than a year. It may be of interest to note that the parish secretary in 1952 was Mrs. Eleanor Mauzy; her funeral was held at Holy Faith fifty years later.

[6] The rector's report for 1956 noted that two other young men from Holy Faith were attending seminary.

"O Taste and See," which had been composed for the coronation of Queen Elizabeth II. In addition to placing more emphasis on the adult choir the new organist also decided to form a Youth Choir for boys and girls in grade seven and up, including those graduating from the Junior Choir. These two groups would alternate in singing for the Family Service. The Junior Choir had been singing more duets rather than solos (the writer probably meant more anthems in two parts rather than one); his was desirable "due to the [rearrangement of the church and the] lightness of the children's voices."

Several Church School classes were divided into two parts in 1955 since it was believed that ten or twelve was the maximum number of students that could be handled in one group. Space remained inadequate and one high school class had to meet in a private dining room at La Posada. More radical changes followed in 1956: "the Church School took a deep breath and decided to organize a second shift," as had been discussed earlier. The first set of classes met from 9:15 to 10:00 with the family worship service from 10:00 to 10:30; then there was a second class period from 10:30 to 11:15. The rector acknowledged that this complex scheduling confused many people, and the report from the Church School admitted that even with the two sessions "our attendance is not too impressive: in the Primary average attendance is about 45-50 in the first shift and 15-20 in the second. In the Secondary Department there are 123 students enrolled in the first shift with an average attendance of 80. In the second shift there are 55 students enrolled and an average attendance of 33."

The 1957 budget anticipated receipts of $41,000 ($36,000 from pledges). The rector was paid $5550, the curate $2450 (for seven months), and the organist $1500 (more than twice the previous part-time stipend of $720). The diocesan assessment and quota was $5774. Among the special funds expended were $227 for theological education, plus $67.30 given to Dean Gray Blandy of the Seminary of the Southwest in Austin when he visited the parish. The Thanksgiving offering of $233 was sent to the San Juan Mission hospital. Holy Faith also contributed $440 to the purse given to Bishop Stoney at the time of his retirement and $217 toward the purchase a new crozier for Bishop Kinsolving. The rector's discretionary fund, composed of gratuities received for performing weddings and funerals, a monthly contribution from the Guild, and individual gifts, amounted to $2225 and was used primarily for loans to those in distress. The Guild provided direct support for the St. Francis Boys' Home in Kansas and St. Michael's Farm for Boys in Mississippi, while the Service Group sent articles for children to the Grenfell Mission in Labrador.

Early in 1956 Holy Faith served as host parish for the diocesan convention. Several parish groups were involved in provided hospitality or handling arrangements. The Altar Guild, for instance, made a frontal for the temporary altar placed in St. Francis Auditorium, where the sessions were held. The senior warden, Brigadier Mordant Ellerington, a British army survivor of the fall of Singapore, presided at several convention functions. The event must have been a poignant homecoming for Bishop Kinsolving, and Father Seaman wrote that "many of our people gained a wider vision of the work of the church."

†

One of Seaman's new enterprises involved the establishment of a Woman's Auxiliary–the name was available since the old Auxiliary had not met for years–which would include all Women of the Church. "Much thought and effort," the rector said, "have gone into [this] effort to expand the work of the Women of the Church and to increase their vision." Such changes in women's work were common through the Episcopal Church in the 1950s. In Santa Fe the program was initiated by the visit of Mrs. Paul R. Palmer of Muskogee, Oklahoma, president of the National Women's Auxiliary, in January 1955. The new Holy Faith Auxiliary was organized in 1956 with Mrs. Albert Lathrop as president and Mrs. John Dendahl as treasurer. The rector was delighted, for this "significant step" meant that "there is a program and a field for service for EVERY woman of the parish." As many as sixty women attended its meetings, but initially they were infrequent. In May 1956 the Rev. Eugene Botelho spoke on the San Juan Mission to the Navajo, which Holy Faith had been supporting for some years. On October 19 Mrs. O. R. Sellers discussed new movements in Christianity, an in December a "quiet hour" included meditations by the Rev. Paul Saunders of Albuquerque. Members of the existing Guild and Service Group seem to have taken this initiative in good stead, at least for the time being; they cooperated to entertain Mrs. Palmer, and the Service Group paid her expenses of $56.50. Faith Meem was then president of the Service Group, which (rather than the Guild) served dinner before the parish meeting in January. For a time the Guild continued to sponsor the bazaar, and its members made calls on new parishioners. The library committee found several new members as the result of a survey of church women conducted by the new Auxiliary.

An additional women's group, St. Mary's Guild, was organized in 1957 to serve those who might prefer to meet in the morning. A babysitter was provided for their gatherings on the second Wednesday of the month, which came to be held in members' homes. During their first year St. Mary's undertook the landscaping of the church patio and decorated Palen Hall for the bazaar. Later the group took a special interest in the School for the Deaf and in 1961 they gave a graduation dress to a deserving woman student there. In 1964, however, the group disbanded, partly because its president had to resign when she accepted a full-time position. Another group, St. Gabriel's Guild, was established in 1960 "with the idea of letting women who have limited time have an opportunity for service, with special emphasis on communication." For several years its members compiled a calendar of events which was appended to the annual parish report and arranged displays, sometimes historical, in the tower room between the church and Palen Hall. In 1960 they handled publicity and hospitality for the Bishop's Players, a group from California which came to Santa Fe to present a dramatized version of C. S. Lewis' book *The Great Divorce*. Two years later the players returned to stage *Winnie the Pooh* and Alan Paton's moving African saga *Cry the Beloved Country*. One of the reports from St. Gabriel's speaks of attempting to explain the customs and beliefs of American Indians to children of the parish, but we hear no more about the project.

In 1961 the Parish Service Guild, which had run the rummage sales for several years, turned them over to the Women of the Church. Two years later it was acknowledged that the Service Guild "was losing ground, so this group chose to elect new officers, reinstill interest in an evening guild," and change its name to St. Hilda's. As another report put it, St. Hilda's replaced the old Service Guild "with new members, a new constitution, and renewed interest; it has been active under the leadership of Mrs. W. R. Buckley." Programs included talks by Mrs. Higham on her travels in Southern Rhodesia, Bishop Kinsolving on diocesan programs, and Myra Ellen Jenkins on the early history of the Episcopal church in New Mexico. In 1964 the forty-six members heard Lillian Rockett describe her travels in Hawaii and Beatrice Chauvenet review the *Book of the Hopi*; Dorothy Lanham was president and program chairman. Members of *The* Guild (since it had been in existence so long it needed no further name) continued to be active during these years but changed their focus after the organization of the Women of the Church: "we have tried to have interesting programs to help replace our former numerous projects," especially the bazaar, the Guild's 1961 report said. There were still annual garden teas, at places like the Bishop's residence[7] and the home of John and Faith Meem, and the group continued to support the Mater-

---

[7] The diocesan headquarters had been moved temporarily from Albuquerque to Santa Fe in the 1960s as a result of a gift of land from Amelia White. This

nal Health Center, St. Francis Boys' Home, and St. Michael's Farm for Boys. There was little change in the Daughters of the King; it remained a small group emphasizing prayer and visits to the sick and shut in. The Women of the Church themselves "quietly saw things fall into a pattern," as their report for 1961 said. Except during the summer they had monthly luncheons with programs, the food being prepared by the smaller groups in rotation, and they continued the traditional rummage sales and December bazaars. One experiment involved holding the bazaar tea in Faith House rather than Palen Hall; it was said to be more elegant in these quieter surroundings, beautifully decorated for the occasion. A final innovation was the attempt to organize a men's group in 1964. John Gaw Meem agreed to serve as chairman. After several planning sessions the men served barbeque to 350 parishioners, at a profit of $250. So far as we know this was the sole project of the Men of Holy Faith.

†

The 1960s saw the installation of a pipe organ. This was long overdue; Holy Faith had been making do with a Hammond electric organ ever since the removal of the old Hook & Hastings instrument. As the new organist Joseph Leonard wrote in 1958, "The Church of the Holy Faith deserves a pipe organ, and it is to be hoped by your present organist that someday in the not too distant future this dream will be realized. There is $6000 set aside for this already. Much is being lost in the way of beautiful music written for the church and the organ, that cannot be played on a Hammond. The worship of Almighty God deserves the best in all endeavors of ours. Could we possibly add this one?" At the time there were only three pipe organs in Santa Fe, two in churches and one in the St. Francis Auditorium.

The dream was not to be realized during Leonard's short tenure, but in 1960 his successor Mark Davis was able to report that a contract had been signed with the M. P. Möller Organ Company of Hagerstown, Maryland, one of the country's largest builders.[8] The tonal consultant for the instrument was Ernest White, who had earlier been one of Davis's teachers. White had designed a number of the

---

provided space for the bishop's residence and office; it resolved tensions between the two cathedral cities, Albuquerque and El Paso, and enabled the Kinsolvings to return to the city they loved. Mary Kinsolving died in February 1969 after suffering a heart attack while supervising young skiers at the Santa Fe Ski Basin. After retiring as diocesan Bishop Kinsolving made his home in Santa Fe and married his second wife, Eleanor, whom he had met while traveling on a vacation. They remained popular at Holy Faith.

country's finest organs and was widely respected; he was not, however, enamored of the English cathedral organ and favored baroque specifications which were more suited to the playing of Bach and other German composers. Since only limited funds were available at Holy Faith, the new organ was small. It had three manuals but only nineteen ranks. Only the Swell organ was enclosed and under expression; the Great and Choir were exposed and displayed on the right-hand side of the chancel. In keeping with White's preferences there was no 8' Diapason or Principal anywhere in the instrument; the Great had a 4' Principal and the Choir a 2'. The only 8' stop on the Great was a Bourdon. There was only one reed (a Trompette on the Swell) and one mixture (a three-rank Plein Jeu, also on the Swell). Preparation was made for additions, however; they were to include a Great mixture and several more reeds on the Swell and Pedal.[9]

To generate enthusiasm for the installation of the new organ Holy Faith sponsored a concert by Francis Jackson, the organist of York Minster in England, at the St. Francis Auditorium in April 1961. There was a full house and, as Mark Davis noted, this was "shades of things to come."[10] The church organ was dedicated during a service of Evensong on January 14, 1962. On March 20 the famous performer and composer Jean Langlais, organist of the church of Ste. Clothilde in Paris, played the opening recital. According to Davis it was "a stunning program." Langlais is said to have called the instrument "la plus jolie que j'avais joué"–he must have meant that the little organ was fun to play; it was a far cry from the great Cavaillé-Coll instrument at Ste. Clothilde, which is often

---

[8] In 1950 John Gaw Meem had suggested that Holy Faith purchase the two-manual pipe organ being removed from St. John's Cathedral in Albuquerque, for which he was constructing a new building. There is no sign that the suggestion generated much enthusiasm. See correspondence in Box I.36, parish archives.

[9] There is a copy of the contract and some related correspondence in the "Organ" file in the parish archives, Box I.36.The author may be permitted to comment that he was involved in the installation of a pipe organ at the Church of the Good Shepherd in Austin, Texas, at almost exactly the same time. He also had a specification proposed by Ernest White but chose a more traditional design drawn up by Franklin Mitchell for the Reuter Organ Company of Lawrence, Kansas. This organ was substantially larger than the one at Holy Faith.

[10] In 1958 Vernon de Tar, the well-known organist from the Church of the Ascension in New York City, played for one of the services, possibly with the hope of interesting parishioners in the prospect of a new organ. During Fiesta week that year "Mr. Leonard's antique pump organ was brought to the church and played for the entire 11 o'clock service. Many liked the old organ better than our Hammond," he said.

thought to possess the world's greatest reed stops—and Davis said that "it was the finest organ, bar none, that this bench-warmer has ever touched." During the summers of 1962 and 1963 there was an organ recital on the first Sunday of each month. Most concerts were by Davis, but Susan Loriaux of the Presbyterian Church also performed. The organ was dedicated to the memory of Helen Hyde, who had died in December 1960. She had contributed some of the funds in the organ account, and others were given as memorials to her. According to the contract the cost of the new instrument was $28,745.

Mark Davis believed that the organ substantially improved congregational singing, but he had to report that during its first summer the senior choir had hit "a frightening slump; illness, prolonged vacations, unexplained and unannounced absences, and perhaps even temporary indifferences all did their part." Fortunately "the late Fall saw a return to normalcy." The practice of having soloists from the Santa Fe Opera sing at services during the summer months had begun in 1958 and may have been one reason why choir members felt that their presence was not essential.[11]

†

The burial office for Helen Hyde was read by Bishop Kinsolving and Fr. Seaman on December 22, 1960. As several persons commented at the time, it was most appropriate that the Christmas decorations were in place, for Mrs. Hyde had been directress of the Altar Guild for many years and of all seasons loved Christmas best. In addition to serving Holy Faith she had been one of the first presidents of the Woman's Auxiliary in the Missionary District, a leader in organizing chapters of the Daughters of the King, and custodian of the United Thank Offering.

Many Holy Faith parishioners remembered her fondly because of her custom of giving silver crosses to members of the Junior Altar Guild and Prayer Books to young men and women on the occasion of their confirmation.[12] Although, according to the report of the Altar Guild in 1960, she "had lived in a very Spartan-like manner on a fixed and meager income," no one had done more for the church.

---

[11] In addition to his work at Holy Faith, Mark Davis was director of the Santa Fe Choral Society, for which he conducted a performance of Bach's St. Matthew Passion.

[12] Some of Mrs. Hyde's notebooks and travel diaries are in the Holy Faith archives, Box II.11.

(32) Helen Hyde, photo courtesy Museum of New Mexico, Neg. No. 7406.

†

Between 1956 and 1965 Holy Faith helped sponsor a nursing home, the House of St. Luke the Physician. For several years a group of parishioners had been interested in the concept of a church-related home providing nursing care and sheltered living. A board was established, with Beatrice Chauvenet serving as president, and a registered nurse, Elizabeth Brooke, was employed as director. According to a brief history written by Father Seaman, "several possible sites were considered, but the one that seemed to be perfect in every respect was the Frances Wilson home on Buena Vista. This home known and loved by everyone in Santa Fe is ideally located in a central but quiet location, well withdrawn from the street." Just off Canyon Road, it had previously been operated as a guest ranch by Major and Mrs. Edward Oakley. Seaman thought that it would need very little conversion to provide space for as many as twelve persons plus accommodation for the staff, and he was pleased that it was being offered by the Wilson heirs at a most attractive price. In a letter to the *New Mexican* the rector emphasized that the home was not to be operated directly by Holy Faith. "The House of St. Luke the Physician is licensed as a non-profit corporation under the auspices of a Board of Trustees," he wrote. "This will be a church related, not a church sponsored institution, with the rector of the Church of the Holy Faith acting as chaplain to the Home." The facilities included a small chapel. Although membership on the Board and admission to the home were open to persons of all faiths, members of Holy Faith always dominated, and several parish organizations visited the residents and helped them in various ways. During her last years Helen Hyde lived at St. Luke's, and it was there that she died. By 1965 Elizabeth Brooke had retired and it had become difficult to find suitable staff, so the board reluctantly decided that the home should be closed. In May the facilities were sold to Dr. Jean Rosenbaum, a psychiatrist, for $31,500, and medical equipment brought in a bit more; after expenses were paid about $23,000 remained, and it was turned over to Holy Faith in accordance with the articles of incorporation.[13]

Another concern of these years was the lack of a college preparatory school in Santa Fe. In 1961 Father Seaman convened a small group of men to consider the possibility of establishing a church-related institution. The project was daunting

---

[13] The records of St. Luke are in the Holy Faith archives, Boxes III.6-7; cf. Beatrice Chauvenet, *Holy Faith in Santa Fe* (Santa Fe, 1977), pp. 56-57. Vestry minutes show that several parishioners, including John Gaw Meem, urged that the funds be used for a retirement facility of some sort, perhaps in the former home of Bronson Cutting, but in the end they went into the building fund.

and was eventually dropped, but these efforts helped prepare the ground for the founding of the Santa Fe Preparatory School a few years later.[14]

✝

In his annual report for 1958 Seaman said that the Church of the Holy Faith had "become landed."

> At the beginning of the year we secured the title to five acres of choice land in the Mateo Heights addition–land that in the near future will provide the site for a second Episcopal Church in Santa Fe. Last summer we received a tract of 1300 acres eight miles southeast of town in the Rancho San Sebastian area–the gift of Miss Flora Conrad. This land is beautifully located in the foothills of the Sangre de Christo mountains and contains great variety of woodlands ranging from cottonwoods to tall pines. Beginning this spring we hope to develop this land as a camping and recreation area for the use of the parish. A committee has been appointed to begin to make plans for the use of this land. Finally in September the Vestry voted to purchase rather than rent a home for our new assistant rector and his family. Accordingly the Church acquired the property at 129 Solano Dr. where the Rev. and Mrs. Bernard L. Short now reside. This purchase threw our 1958 budget out of kilter, but it was felt to be a good investment and we were able to make this purchase without having to increase our mortgage on the church property in order to raise the down payment.

Discussions of founding a mission or second Episcopal parish in Santa Fe went back to the years when Kinsolving was rector. It was frequently suggested that this should take place when the communicant strength of Holy Faith reached a thousand, but in the end the church did not wait that long. Land on the south side of Santa Fe, including a strip fronting on St. Francis Drive, was purchased in 1958. It was a good location, for subsequent housing development was to lead to the growth of that area. The new mission was established in 1962, partly as a result of the determination of the priest who was serving as assistant at Holy Faith. As we have seen, Seaman felt that an assistant rector was needed, and he

---

[14] Chauvenet, p. 57. Seaman may have been inspired by the success of a similar institution, St. Stephen's School in Austin, Texas, which had been founded under the leadership of Bishop John Hines.

was briefly helped by Norman Riebe. After Riebe's departure and a year's interim the Rev. Bernard Short (mentioned above) served for about two years. Following another year's vacancy the Rev. William E. Crews answered Holy Faith's call, but it was understood from the beginning that his real mission was the foundation of a new church. Some members of Holy Faith were glad enough to see him go, for they regarded his views as being too liberal. Sixty families—178 individual communicants—transferred from Holy Faith to form the initial congregation of the mission; within six months there were eighty families. At the suggestion of Col. John W. Chapman the new church was named St. Bede's, honoring the Venerable historian of the early English church. Initially its meetings were held in a lodge hall on Cerrillos Road, but soon a chapel was built on the land donated by Holy Faith. St. Bede's was officially recognized by the diocese in January 1963. As Beatrice Chauvenet wrote, "The division of the parish was accomplished without open animosity, but the loss of sixty families—many of them young people who chose to follow the dynamic young priest—was costly to the old parish."[15] Relations between the two churches have always been somewhat strained, partly because the younger parish came to favor less traditional liturgy and theology than its forebear. Still, Seaman said, "We welcome them as a sister congregation, not forgetting that once they were daughters."

The land donated by Flora Conrad was to become the site of Camp Stoney, named for James M. Stoney following the bishop's death. In 1963 Seaman reported that a well was being drilled on the property, and when the water supply proved acceptable the land was given to the diocese for use as a camp, available for young people's gatherings and adult retreats and recreation. At first the only building was a former cow barn; it was turned into a chapel but retained some of the aroma of its former occupants. A swimming pool was installed and named in honor of Mary Kinsolving, the bishop's wife who had died in February 1969. After improvements were made the parish benefitted by being able to use the facilities for parish picnics and, of course, by being able to send young people to summer camps.

More important for the parish was the project of building a new educational building. In his annual report for 1962 Father Seaman said that a major effort for the year would be the establishment of a building fund, so that proper classrooms might replace the space in Faith House, the old rectory which still stood behind the church. The building program was postponed for a year or two, since Holy Faith was contributing to the Diocesan Advancement Fund as well as to the

---

[15] Chauvenet, pp. 55-56.

(33) Mary Vilura Conkey residence designed by John Gaw Meem in 1927, Holy Faith rectory from 1963 to 1985, photo courtesy Center for Southwest Research, University of New Mexico, No. 000-675/091-045M.

founding of St. Bede's, but the time came when (as the rector wrote) "having considered the needs of others, we must now face our own." It was the generosity of Mary Vilura Conkey that finally made the building possible. After many years of serving Holy Faith in various capacities she died in 1963; since she had no direct heirs, she gave her home to Holy Faith and, after a few minor bequests, designated the parish as her residual legatee.[16]

Miss Conkey's residence had been designed by her friend John Gaw Meem in 1927. Built near the Sunmount Sanitorium, where both had been patients, it was one of the finest early examples of the architect's work and displayed many elements of what came to be known as the Santa Fe style—vigas, latillas, balustrades, corner fireplaces, beautifully carved doors, portals, and a patio.[17] Miss

---

[16] John Gaw Meem was one of Miss Conkey's executors. As she had wished, 10% of her bequest to the church was sent to the diocese.

[17] For a description of the house, and photographs of it, see Chris Wilson, *Facing Southwest: The Life and Houses of John Gaw Meem* (New York, 2001), pp. 135-139. It was located on a dirt lane which subsequently became Camino de la Cruz Blanca; one of the parish's first expenses was a bill for paving.

Conkey's will stipulated that Holy Faith should use the house for church purposes for at least twenty-one years, after which it might be disposed of if necessary. It was thought to be large enough to house a rector and also provide rooms for student activities, perhaps by students at St. John's College; a small chapel might be fitted up as well. Father Seaman never lived there, but his assistant and his successor did.[18] Eventually the parish decided that a different rectory might be desirable and agreed to sell the house to the Meems, members of whose family still occupy it. It remains one of Santa Fe's most beautiful buildings.

It was the new educational building, not the residence, that came to be known as Conkey House. Seaman's report for 1964 noted that the building fund had benefitted from the "sizable bequest" from the Conkey estate. This amounted to $69,039, and the building fund held an additional $38,159. Construction did not begin during Seaman's tenure as rector, however, and the actual building forms part of the next chapter in the history of the parish.

†

Despite these accomplishments the early 1960s brought a series of problems. The number of baptized members reached a peak of 1371 in 1961 but, partly because of transfers to St. Bede's, had declined to 1034 by 1964. The number of Church School students fell from 312 to 196, the year's total attendance from 26,381 to 21,179. There were financial difficulties as well. Some of these arose simply from the generosity of the parish; for much of this period the funds given to the diocese and to other outside organizations were as large as or larger than the sums expended locally. In 1962, according to the annual report, "the problems of the vestry were complicated by the purchase of the Hyde Memorial Organ. The total cost of the organ and chamber was $36,000, half of which was in hand in cash, and the vestry anticipated the other half coming from the Hyde bequest which was assigned for that purpose. Unexpected delays in receiving these funds caused the vestry to borrow both from the bank and from special funds in order to meet the organ payments." There were also some complications about the bequests by Miss Conrad and Miss Conkey, as well as unpaid pledges.

Then there was the difficulty of finding and retaining assistant rectors. As we have seen, the Revs. Riebe, Short, and Crews had tenures of two years or less. In 1963 Seaman lamented that "after a number of years of being the 'executive type' with an assistant to share the work, to be without a fellow worker for a year and a half demands a re-adjustment of one's schedule. One can get spoiled." The

---

[18] See Chauvenet, pp. 58-59.

rector had also been busy as President of the New Mexico Council of Churches. He hoped that group would soon be able to employ a full-time executive secretary, and he looked forward to the arrival of a new assistant, Alfred C. Krader, who was coming from El Paso. Krader was thought to be a fine teacher and preacher, and since he would be living in Miss Conkey's house near St. John's "we can anticipate the college becoming an increasing portion of the mission of the parish as it grows in size." Krader assumed his position in May 1964, and in November the vestry was told that he was taking charge of the 9:00 family service and had in mind making changes "in the length of the service and other matters." But he soon experienced differences of opinion with the rector, and in February 1965 Seaman announced Krader's resignation and request for three months' terminal pay. Bishop Kinsolving then met with the vestry for a lengthy discussion of "the theological and other matters involved in the assistant rector's resignation." There was a compromise about terminal pay, and Krader was allowed to stay in the Conkey residence until March 1, "at which time he is supposed to report on his new position." He left Holy Faith complaining that his car allowance had not been properly paid.

Krader's departure triggered discussion of Seaman's position as well. At the meeting attended by the bishop the senior warden presented a statement urging the rector to "make full use of lay participation through the vestry. We ask the rector to work with us so that we may in turn work fully with him." It was suggested specifically that a new Sunday School superintendent should be named, that the women's group should be free to elect its own slate of officers, and that the building committee should be reactivated, evidently a sign that the rector was thought to be interfering inappropriately in these areas. What was not said directly was that Seaman had become greatly impressed by the director of the parish youth program, Phyllis Snow, the wife of an obstetrician. Mrs. Snow believed that she was receiving messages from the Virgin Mary and she passed them on to the rector, who discussed them publicly. Disturbed by all this, the vestry voted to dismiss Mrs. Snow and became critical of Father Seaman.

The breach came in February 1965, when the vestry unanimously adopted a resolution calling for Seaman's resignation. "In view of the vestry's lack of confidence in the rector's ability to weld the parish together after the serious incidents occurring in recent weeks," it read, "it is the vestry's suggestion that the rector seek another assignment." The vestry minutes record agreement that no one should speak a word of the resolution until the bishop had been consulted, but that undertaking was not honored. Stephen Watkins, then one of the newer members of the vestry, remembers going home from the meeting only to be confronted within fifteen minutes by an angry Dr. Snow. Pacing up and down the living room in a great rage while Watkins' wife and children cowered in a corner, Snow said that the vestry was doing terrible things to Seaman. Watkins tried to make peace, and evidently he succeeded, since the following Sunday found him and Snow side by side at the communion rail.[19] On March 2 it was reported that the rector "appeared to be actively seeking a new position," and on March 18 he submitted his resignation, effective April 1. According to the vestry minutes "Rev. Seaman reported on his special interest in alcoholism in a metropolitan area and the plans he was making to devote his full time to such activities." On leaving Santa Fe he went first to Phoenix, but he soon found his way to the West Coast, where became associated with the controversial bishop James Pike.[20] Despite his early successes his years at Holy Faith had ended abruptly and tragically.

---

[19] I am grateful to Watkins for sharing his memories of this occasion.

[20] Vestry minutes, 1964-1965, Box I.9, parish archives. Herman Barkmann was senior warden, Paul Franke junior warden, and Stephen Watkins clerk of the vestry. Seaman later served in Washington state and was listed in 2000 as a retired priest of the diocese of Olympia. *Episcopal Church Annual 2000* (Harrisburg, Pa., 2000), pp. 277, C126.

8. "The Graveyard of Clergy," 1965-1972

In 1936 C. J. Kinsolving had been warned that he should be wary of accepting the call to Holy Faith, since the parish was known as "the graveyard of the Episcopal clergy."[1] As we have seen, Kinsolving himself did not find it so; both he and the parish prospered under his leadership. But it may be true that Holy Faith was more given to disagreements about churchmanship, liturgical style, and theology than most parishes, and that these became increasingly bitter in later years when the national church was struggling which such divisive issues as Prayer Book revision, the ordination of women priests, and more active social policies. Certainly the period from 1965 to 1972 was in many ways an unsettled one for the church in Santa Fe. Dissension deepened; clergy served for relatively short periods and experienced difficulties of various sorts.[2]

As we have seen, Henry F. Seaman resigned as rector in the Spring of 1965 after having served the parish just over a decade. Since his departure was sudden, it was not possible to have his successor in place immediately, and the Rev. George A. Stracke served as *locum tenens* for several months. To guide them in their search for a permanent rector the vestry adopted a set of proposed qualifications. The clergyman chosen, they agreed, should be between 35 and 50 years of age,

---

[1] Quoted in Beatrice Chauvenet, *Holy Faith in Santa Fe* (Santa Fe, 1977), p. 48. Chauvenet attributed the remark to "a woman representing the national organization of the Woman's Auxiliary of the Episcopal Church."

[2] As usual this chapter relies heavily on annual parish reports, but they are less full and helpful than in earlier years. In particular they do not include annual reports of the rector; he must have continued to make comments at each annual meeting, but if they were written down they do not survive. The vestry minutes have also been consulted, but they are formal and rarely contain summaries of discussion.

preferably married, ideally with some experience in a field outside the church, a "middle-of-the-road 'prayer book' churchman, sound in doctrine and liturgy but neither excessively high nor low church and preferably coming from a seminary of such views as the Episcopal Theological Seminary at Cambridge, Massachusetts; Bexley Hall, Gambier, Ohio; University of the South at Sewanee; Episcopal Theological Seminary of the Southwest at Austin, Texas, and Virginia Theological Seminary." He should have a strong interest in youth and in parish development and be willing to delegate authority to lay persons. "The question of whether he should be a liberal or conservative in theological matters was not dwelt upon [by the vestry] because of the shortage of time, but a conservative rather than one excessively liberal would appear to be more acceptable to the majority of the vestry."[3]

On June 8 the vestry discussed the possible candidates and voted unanimously to inform Bishop Kinsolving that they wished to call the Rev. Richard H. Williams, canon of St. John's Cathedral in Albuquerque, to be the new rector. Arrangements were soon completed and Williams moved to Santa Fe with his wife Cherald and their three daughters. They made their home in the residence bequeathed to Holy Faith by Mary Vilura Conkey.

As Beatrice Chauvenet, who was an active member of the parish at the time, commented in her history of Holy Faith, "There had been division in the church at the time of Mr. Seaman's departure and regrettably it continued under Mr. Williams."[4] Statistics (see Appendix I) show that the total annual attendance at services continued to decline, as it had since 1962, reaching a low of 14,629 in 1966. There were also budgetary problems, and the vestry wrestled with ways of increasing revenue or cutting expenses.[5] At the vestry meeting held on July 5, 1967, only two years after his appointment, Father Williams submitted his resignation. Health problems being experienced by members of his family were the stated reason, but other disaffections must have been present as well. Accepting the resignation, the senior warden, Paul R. Franke, Jr., wrote Williams that "if it were in the power of this vestry to reverse your decision, we would make every effort to do so, knowing your departure will be an irreplaceable loss for the entire parish." Stephen Watkins, already active at Holy Faith, believed that Williams

---

[3] Vestry minutes, April 7, 1965, parish archives, Box I.9.
[4] Chauvenet, p. 58.
[5] See vestry minutes, especially November 15, 1966: Box I.9, parish archives. Stephen Watkins remembers the Every Member Canvasses of this period. In 1965 some said they would not give until the parish got rid of Seaman; in 1966 some said they would not give because the parish had dismissed him.

was a fine young man but that he found himself unable to deal with entrenched parish leaders who were conservative in their politics, low church in their religious views, and accustomed to running things in their own way.[6] In 1966 Williams had been able to persuade the Rev. Dennis Walker to come from Alaska to be his assistant; Walker, his wife Carol, and their three children moved to Santa Fe in May. A native of Whittier, California, Walker had attended Stanford University and the Church Divinity School of the Pacific. Upon Williams' resignation the vestry considered nine candidates for his position, and according to their minutes there was "very much discussion" before it was unanimously agreed to promote Walker to the position of rector. He held the office until January 1972.

Walker's years were not easy either. He fell out with both of his assistants. In 1968 he employed the Rev. Harold Edmonson of Rockport, Texas, to be assistant rector, but Edmonson left after only ten months. He had been placed in charge of Christian education and youth work at what Chauvenet called "a very difficult time for young people. Permissiveness in the attitude of parents and educators toward teen-agers was resulting in general unrest and tension. Riots on college campuses [the anti-war demonstrations of the Viet Nam era] and resentment of authority generally gave evidence of changing philosophies. Some devout people insisted that all the old moral values had changed. Father Edmonson found that disagreement among the parishioners made it almost impossible to carry out his work as he saw it."[7]

Edmonson was replaced by the Rev. Elvin R. Gallagher, whom Walker had known in Alaska. Gallagher's wife Margaret and their four children accompanied him to Santa Fe. Since it was difficult to find suitable rental properties, the church bought a house at 650 Paseo de la Cuma, near the Old Cross of the Martyrs (not the present Cross on Fort Marcy Hill), to be their residence. Gallagher was popular with the young people, who nicknamed him "Big." In December 1969 the teen-agers of Holy Faith and St. Bede's (a group of 46 in all) went to Denver for an "exposure experience" arranged by Fr. John Kinsolving of St. Bede's; according to Gallagher it was most rewarding. A year later, however, Gallagher ended the practice of having the youth of the two parishes meet jointly—"nothing precipitated the move," he said, "just a difference of ideas in what our groups wanted to participate in."[8] In June 1970 fifteen young people from Holy Faith went with Gallagher on a trip to Colorado and the Navajo reservation. They rode

---

[6] I am grateful to Mr. Watkins for sharing these views with me.
[7] Chauvenet, p. 61. In 2000 Edmonson was retired and living in Roswell.
[8] Gallagher's annual report for the year 1970, parish archives.

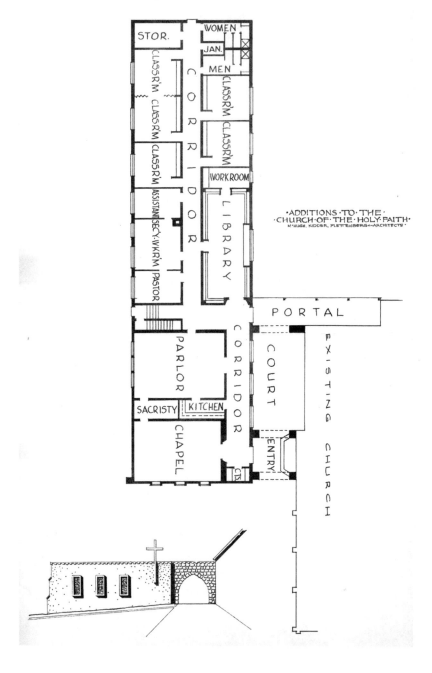

(34) Plan for additions to Church of the Holy Faith (Conkey House) by McHugh, Kidder, Plettenberg Architects, parish archives, Box II.16.

the narrow-gauge railroad from Durango to Silverton, toured Mesa Verde National Park, and stayed with the Indians at Carson's Post. Paul Franke, an adult who accompanied the youth, told the vestry that "he had the highest praise for the conduct of the teen-agers, and he commented on their opportunity for a contrast of worship services with the Holy Communion at St. Mark's Church in Durango, which is a very high church, and in the St. Luke's chapel at Carson's Post on the reservation."[9]

Gallagher also organized a successful Vacation Bible School and his wife put her musical abilities to good use by singing in the choir. But in June 1970 the vestry noted that Sunday School attendance was down (there were only 86 students registered) and Gallagher was directed to visit young parishioners to determine why the did not attend the family service regularly. This was perhaps one reason for the rift between the rector and his assistant, and Gallagher too presented his resignation after little more than two years at Holy Faith. His farewell letter to members of the Library Guild suggests something of his character. "Thank you more than I can ever express for all the labor of love you have given to your church in your service in this place," he wrote. "In turn you have given to me much to be grateful for in the beauty of good books but much more in being able to take into my heart your friendship."[10] In 1971 the Gallaghers moved to Boise, Idaho, where he became rector of All Saints Church.[11] According to the annual report of the Holy Faith Guild "an extraordinarily large crowd" attended the farewell potluck supper on February 19.

✝

Soon after Father Williams' formal installation as rector on September 22, 1965, the vestry finished negotiating a contract for the construction of the new educational building. It was to be located just west of the church, on a piece of land which the parish had purchased from the Zook estate, and in addition to classrooms it would contain office space, a lounge, a library, and a chapel. The architect was Bradley P. Kidder, a parishioner and a member of the firm of McHugh, Kidder, and Plettenberg. His partner John McHugh was also a member of Holy Faith and consulted about the project, as did John Gaw Meem, who took an active interest although he was now retired from active architectural

[9] Vestry minutes, June 25, 1970, parish archives, Box I.10.
[10] Holy Faith Library annual report for 1971, parish archives.
[11] In 2000 he was still living in Boise but had retired.

practice himself.[12] Both McHugh and Kidder were "Meem men" and had formerly worked in his office.[13]

The original plans called for a two-story building, the upper floor providing rooms for Church School classes, but when the cost was estimated at more than $200,000 this was thought to be more than the parish could afford and the second story was eliminated. According to Stephen Watkins, one of the vestrymen commented that since there were practically no Sunday School students there was no need for the upper floor. (The actual number of pupils was then 121, less than half of what it had been six or seven years earlier.)[14] A few other changes were made after consultation with parishioners and staff members. It had originally been planned to have the chapel adjacent to the building's main entrance and the library at the south end, but in the end these locations were reversed. It is interesting to note that Meem regarded the transposition as a significant improvement: he liked "the location of the library close to the main parking area" and "the location of the chapel directly opposite the West entrance to the church." In general, he wrote, "the plans and specifications please me very much." He did "strongly urge that the portal, north of the chancel, be enclosed in glass and heated. This will enable warm and sheltered communication between the new and the old parts in winter time and will unite the whole structure. It will make an excellent vestibule directly off the parking lot, enabling children to keep warm while waiting to be picked up."[15] Bishop Kinsolving also argued for a covered and heated passageway between the two buildings, but because of the expense involved the vestry decided to postpone such construction for a year. In fact it was never undertaken, but there are attractive arches linking the church and the chapel. It was possible to take stone from the same quarry near Lamy that provided stone

---

[12] Documents and papers relating to the construction of the building are in the parish archives, Box I.47.

[13] Plans for Conkey House may be found in the Meem archives, Southwest Research Center, University of New Mexico, Box 1, folder 12-24. There are also reports from the Albuquerque Testing Laboratories regarding the soundness of the soil beneath the church and the new structure, a matter of some interest because inadequate foundations caused trouble in later years. See also Beatrice Chauvenet, *John Gaw Meem, Pioneer in Historic Preservation* (Santa Fe, 1985), pp. 99-100.

[14] The annual report for 1965 noted that there were too few young children for the usual four classes in the primary department, so they met in one group.

[15] Meem to Richard H. Williams, October 12, 1965, parish archives. Ruth Heflin, the parish bookkeeper, had commented that the allocation of office space was inadequate, but she too was satisfied with the revised plans. Miss Heflin was also Meem's office manager.

for the original church building and, probably, for St. Francis Cathedral. The final agreed cost, including some modifications to Palen Hall and the parking lot, was $189,800. The contractor, J. R. Brennand of the Brennand Construction Company, was like the architect an active member of the church. He had come to Santa Fe from El Paso and served Holy Faith for more than twenty years; he was senior warden when he died suddenly in October 1969 and, as the vestry minutes noted, would be greatly missed throughout the diocese. A scholarship fund was established in his memory to aid in paying the expenses of seminary students from the parish.

It had always been planned that Faith House, the former rectory just north of the church, would be razed when the new building was completed, but in the end this took place more suddenly than had been anticipated. Faith House was demolished in November 1965 when it was declared to be unfit for occupancy. Members of the library committee were given only twenty-four hours' notice that all their books had to be moved to a temporary space in Palen Hall, and (according to their report) "the move was accomplished in a day and a half."[16] Sunday School classes also had to be accommodated unexpectedly in makeshift spaces. The library then had 2579 books valued at $6630; 88 volumes had been added during the year, and more than 900 books had been borrowed.

The new building was called Conkey House and dedicated to the memory of the woman who had done so much to make it possible. In addition to offices, classrooms, and an attractive lounge (later known as the Kinsolving Room) it provided a large, elegant space for the parish library, a sign that this was recognized as being an important part of the life of the parish, and a chapel to be used for weekday services and small weddings. Known as the Chapel of the Good Shepherd in recognition of the original name of the parish, it was dedicated to the memory of T. H. McIlvain, a prominent businessman whose widow (at the suggestion of Stephen Watkins) made a significant contribution to the building fund, and Agnes Wheelwright. The figure originally displayed above the altar, a contemporary representation of the Good Shepherd, was designed by Donna Quasthoff and cast in Nambe ware as a gift of the foundry. The baptismal font was given by Bishop Kinsolving in memory of his wife Mary.[17] The original stained glass windows, abstract in style, were created by Maurice Loriaux, but in 2001 they were replaced by new windows designed by Shaw, a parishioner, artist,

---

[16] Marion Wasson contributed $100 of her own money to pay for the moving expenses.
[17] It was designed by Andrea Bacigalupa and made by the Southwest Spanish Craftsmen.

and former monk who preferred to use only his last name. These depict the Virgin Mary accompanied by a likeness of Shaw's own dog and two medieval English saints, Julian of Norwich (with her cat) and Hugh of Lincoln (with a swan). Loriaux's windows in the corridor from the chapel to the library remain.[18]

†

The women's organizations of the parish found the later years of the 1960s uneasy. Upon becoming rector Father Williams met with the Women of the Church to re-evaluate their usefulness and part in the life of the church. There was talk of restructuring the women's groups into areas of interest, but this was not done. In 1966 the president, Lois Franke, regretted that they had not been able to involve more women–"our year has not been the complete success we might have hoped for," she wrote. The following year a questionnaire was mailed to all the women of Holy Faith to determine the areas of service which might interest them, but few replies were received.

In 1971 the average attendance at meetings of the Women of the Church was thirty-five, while about twenty-four came to gatherings of the Holy Faith Guild. Both groups met monthly except in the summer. Father Williams had hoped to interest them in Moral Rearmament but the actual programs were perhaps more interesting. They included slides of Spain in Holy Week shown by Alan Vedder, the prominent curator of the Spanish Colonial Art collection, and Mrs. Vedder, talks by John Gaw Meem on missionary work in Brazil and on the Old Santa Fe Association, Mr. Gallagher's discussion of the church in Alaska, Myra Ellen Jenkins' description of the new State Archives Center, and a program on the Museum of Navajo Ceremonial Art (later the Wheelwright Museum) by its curator Richard Lang. The women helped pay the assistant rector's salary and continued to make their usual contributions to missions and charities, as well as buying a new dishwasher for the kitchen in Palen Hall and assisting a parish family "in a time of deepest need." For a short time they tried selling Amway products as a means of making money, but this was dropped in favor of continuing the usual rummage sales and annual bazaar, which could be counted on to bring in at least $2000. For several years the women made a hundred pies annu-

---

[18] Chauvenet commented (p. 59) that "for some years the chapel was kept open day and night, shut off by locked gates from the rest of Conkey House when the church offices were closed, but this place of refuge and prayer was damaged by vandals in the early 1970s and the altar littered by the remnants of picnic lunches," so it had to be locked.

[19] Information and quotations from annual reports.

ally to raise funds for St. Vincent's Hospital.[19]

At the annual meeting held on January 24, 1967, the parish voted to amend its by-laws by allowing women to serve as members of the vestry. This had been allowed by action of the diocesan convention the previous spring. The first woman to be elected was Mrs. Jack Woodard, who served for several years as clerk. She was soon followed by Mrs. Brennand and Mrs. Meem.

✝

There were also changes in the music department. Mark Davis, who had been organist and choirmaster throughout much of Father Seaman's tenure, left Holy Faith in 1966. He was succeeded by Mary Jean Cook, whose husband, Dr. Edward Cook, a dentist, was elected to the vestry in 1970 and later served as senior warden. In 1967 Mrs. Cook asked to have her salary reduced, perhaps because she did not wish the responsibilities of what might approach a full-time position; the vestry accordingly voted that she should be paid $150 a month, only half of what Davis had been receiving.[20] Then she requested that James Barber be hired as her assistant and choir director. If this was done the arrangement did not last long. Mrs. Ruth Rye served as organist in 1968 but resigned early in 1969; Mrs. Cook agreed to return as organist until a replacement could be found, and Dr. Cook was named chairman of the music committee of the vestry. A musician from Borger, Texas, Cleve Redman, was contacted about the position but in the end was not interested in coming to Santa Fe, so Mrs. Cook remained at the console. The youth choir appears to have flourished; in September 1969 Dr. Cook reported that the number of children exceeded the number of vestments available. He added that he and Mrs. Cook planned to be in Europe for three weeks

---

[20] Mrs. Cook was asked to decide whether an electric reed organ offered to the church for use in the chapel should be accepted but found that it was not in good enough condition. A historian as well as a musician, Mary Jean Cook is the author of two important studies of the Loretto Chapel, the newer of which (*Loretto: The Sisters and Their Santa Fe Chapel*, published in 2002) succeeds in identifying the builder of the supposedly miraculous stairway. The Cooks lived in one of John Gaw Meem's finest houses. Surrounded by thirty acres of piñon forest off the Camino San Acacio, it had been built for the New York heiress Amelia Hollenback, whose letters Mrs. Cook later edited, and contained architectural details taken from historic Indian pueblos and Hispanic villages. Miss Hollenback seldom lived in the house and when she decided to sell it Meem recommended the Cooks as purchasers who could be relied on to retain its historic character. They also owned the historic Spiegelberg house a block west of Holy Faith, now the home of the Peyton-Wright Gallery.

and hoped to hear some fine choirs. During their absence Sam Johnson would handle the music at Holy Faith, and on her return Mrs. Cook would prepare the combined choirs for a performance of Benjamin Britten's church opera "Noye's Fludde." In February 1970 several choir members attended a vestry meeting to present their views about the music program. There was discussion about which choir should sing at which service and whether the youth and adult groups should sometimes be combined, but no decision was reached and it was agreed that the choir director should use her own discretion. A room in Palen Hall had been made available for use by the choirs, evidently none too soon. In June 1970 Mrs. Cook offered to remain as organist without receiving a salary, so that funds would be available for sheet music, soloists, and the completion of the organ, but the vestry took no action. The situation appeared somewhat unsettled during Father Walker's last years as rector.

✝

One of the earliest signs of dissent from the policies of the national church appeared in 1969. Two years earlier the General Convention Special Program had been established with funds given by the national church and the Episcopal Church Women (from their United Thank Offering). The program's aim was "to help the poor and disenfranchised, particularly the black and brown communities, gain social, political and economic power in order to have an effective voice in the decisions which affect their lives." The most controversial of all the GCSP grants was that given to Alianza, a Hispanic organization in New Mexico. This group had laid claim to thirty-five million acres of state land in New Mexico and Texas and launched a virtual guerilla war against forest rangers and other government officials. The National Guard had been called in to restrain its members; their leader, Reies Lopez Tijerina had been sent to prison. In June a special meeting of the Holy Faith vestry was called to consider the Episcopal Church's support for the Alianza. These present, including Fr. Walker, Brennand, Cook, and Mrs. Woodard, were unanimously opposed, as their strong resolution makes clear.

> RESOLVED [it read], that the Church of the Holy Faith . . . is unalterably opposed to the contribution by the Episcopal Church of any amounts of money or other things of material value to the Alianza Federal De Los Pueblos Libros, or to Reies Lopez Tijerina or any organization with which he may be connected, for any purpose whatsoever, as being most detrimental to the area, and as a contribution to the destruction of lawful and socially desirable in-

stitutions.

FURTHER RESOLVED: Requests such as those made by Mr. Tijerina and the Alianza are much the same as blackmail in that honoring such requests contributes to their ability to promote claims for which there is no basis in fact or law, and to consider such requests is doing a great disservice not only to the Church, but to the many law-respecting Spanish Americans in the State of New Mexico.[21]

The matter was raised again at the annual parish meeting in January 1970. Members of Holy Faith were addressed by Mr. William Ikard of La Union, New Mexico, a member of the Executive Council of the national church. He reported that the General Convention which had met at Seattle had designated three million dollars to be expended to meet the crisis in American society by aiding the poor and minority groups. Subsequently the Executive Council had voted to approve a grant to Tijerina's Alianza. This was awarded over the protest of Bishop Kinsolving and a special committee from the diocese which included Dr. Myra Ellen Jenkins of Holy Faith, who was serving as historiographer of the diocese. According to Mrs. Woodard's minutes "a lively discussion followed Mr. Ikard's talk, and the consensus of opinion among the congregation was in solid support of the Bishop's stand in opposing the grant."[22]

Dr. Clifford Morehouse, president of the House of Deputies in the General Convention, later explained that he had been assured that "however violent the Alianza might seem to be, there is nothing in their corporate declarations to say that they *advocate* violence–so, we were told, they qualify under our criteria. Thus, despite strenuous objections and documented arguments by the Bishop and diocesan leaders of New Mexico, we granted the Alianza $40,000 with no strings attached." It is perhaps not surprising that Bishop Kinsolving decided that the diocese retaliate by halting its support of the national church and refusing to pay its quota of $82,365. This was the beginning of a long-standing conflict between the diocese and the national church which remained unresolved at the end of the century.[23]

---

[21] Vestry minutes.

[22] Annual report for 1970, parish archives.

[23] For background on this matter see David W. Sumner, *The Episcopal Church's History: 1945-1985* (Wilton, Connecticut, 1987), pp. 50-51.

This issue was only one of the problems facing Holy Faith.[24] As Beatrice Chauvenet wrote, "tension had been mounting among parishioners who once again were divided in their partisanship."[25] What she was too discreet to say was that the rector was in the process of leaving his wife so that he might marry his secretary. Realizing that this would make the continuation of Father Walker's work in Santa Fe difficult, Bishop Kinsolving arranged for him to become a canon of the cathedral in Albuquerque and to help with the foundation of a new church in the suburb of Rio Rancho. He left Holy Faith early in 1972.

---

[24] We may note in passing a relatively insignificant matter which arose in 1971. The County Clerk of Santa Fe County had issued a statement saying that valid marriages could only be performed in the county where the marriage license had been issued. In fact it had been common for couples to obtain a license in one county and have the marriage solemnized in another; Father Walker wrote the state Attorney General, David Norvell, that "If the County Clerk of the County of Santa Fe is correct, then I have performed a number of illegal marriages." Norvell's deputy Oliver E. Payne responded that Walker had done nothing wrong; "Clearly no requirement is imposed that a marriage ceremony must be performed in the county in this state wherein the marriage license was obtained." Correspondence filed in the parish archives with the vestry minutes for 1971.

[25] Chauvenet, p. 62.

9. Fr. Campbell and the Quest for Unity, 1972-1985

Fr. Walker's last Sunday at Holy Faith was January 16, 1972. His successor, the Rev. Donald L. Campbell, became rector on February 1. According to Stephen Watkins, Bishop Kinsolving told the vestry, "You've chewed up three good men. I'm sending you Don Campbell and I don't want to hear from you again for five years!" In fact Campbell was to remain in Santa Fe until 1985.

Fr. Campbell had been born in Butler, Pennsylvania, in 1925. After his high school graduation in May 1943 he was accepted in the U.S. Naval Reserve; he attended midshipman schools in Chicago and Philadelphia and was commissioned an Ensign in May 1943. After the end of World War II he remained in the reserves until the demands of church and family became overwhelming. He worked as a journalist at his home town newspaper for ten years, but he wished to enter the ministry and studied nights and weekends at a seminary in Pittsburgh. He served two parishes in Pittsburgh before he came to New Mexico in 1964 as rector of the Church of the Holy Spirit in Gallup. In 1967 he moved to Albuquerque as a canon of St. John's Cathedral. His family included his wife Kathryn and their three children, Rebecca, then 19, Jonathan, 16, and Jacqueline, 13. He was installed as rector with grand ecclesiastical ceremony on February 27. Both Bishop Kinsolving and Bishop Richard M. Trelease, Jr., who had succeeded him at the beginning of the year, were present; this was the first service of institution conducted by Trelease since becoming bishop. Prior to the institution John B. Haverland, dean of the cathedral in Albuquerque, officiated at Evening Prayer, assisted by the Revs. John Kinsolving of St. Bede's, Fernando Salazar of Española, and Robert Dinegar of Los Alamos.[1] The joint choirs of Holy Faith and St.

---

[1] This was the beginning of Fr. Dinegar's long involvement with Holy Faith. A

John's Cathedral sang under the direction of the Rev. Canon Geoffrey Butcher, organist of the cathedral, who had grown up at Holy Faith. Representatives of the Catholic and Presbyterian churches joined the ecclesiastical procession; the Women of the Church held a reception following the ceremonies.[2]

In his first annual report, delivered at the parish meeting in January 1973, Fr. Campbell said that "The Church of the Holy Faith turned another corner in its relatively long history just a year ago when yet another priest assumed the mantle of spiritual leadership. Even by Holy Faith's rather interesting historical standards, the latest change was rather unusual. It was almost like a spring trade in baseball—Walker to Albuquerque and Campbell to Santa Fe! The usual custom of interviewing a flock of men and finally selecting one you hold would be the right one went by the board in this instance." He was able to look back on a year which had been good in many ways. The acceptance of the rector and his family had been warm and generous. The church's income had exceeded expectations. Attendance was fairly good, "but as we look at Holy Faith in its past with the astonishing attendance figures when the city was much smaller, we have no room for complacency or inordinate pride. We have a long way to go even to get back to where you were twelve or thirteen years ago."[3] Parishioners needed to maintain their lovely plant, to come into a loving relationship with each other, and to glorify and love their Lord. "Of paramount importance is the need for binding us together into a true community. This does not mean we won't disagree, we will. But it does mean that no disagreement will rend the bond of love that unites us in Christ. To attain this ideal it is necessary for us to have a spirit of long-suffering, patience, mutual respect, and a deep love to overcome our human differences. It is not easy, but the alternative of bickering, battling, back-biting, quarreling and other manifestations of human pride is so hideous that it has to be the devil's

---

physical chemist employed in the national laboratory at Los Alamos, Dr. Dinegar had become interested in the church and was trained for ordination as deacon and then priest by the Rev. William Frey, rector of the church of Trinity-on-the-Hill in Los Alamos and later Bishop of Colorado. He later served as an associate priest at both Los Alamos and Holy Faith. He was one of the scientists asked to examine the Shroud of Turin for authenticity and date.

[2] Santa Fe *New Mexican*, February 1 and 27, 1972. Unless otherwise noted the materials used in this chapter come from the files of annual reports and vestry minutes in the parish archives, Boxes I.5, I.10, and I.11.

[3] Rector's reports 1972-1979, filed with annual parish reports, parish archives, Box I.5. Attendance figures may be found in Appendix I below. They had peaked in 1959 with a total annual attendance of 27,154. In 1971 the figure was less than half of that, only 12,669.

work."

This desire to maintain unity at a time when divisive issues separated factions within the church was to underlie much of Campbell's work in Santa Fe. It comes out in most of his annual reports to the parish. In 1974 he said that the church "should teach us to be more loving, more accepting, less critical and judgmental, less harsh in our dealings with others, more spiritual and more joyous." The next year he commented on disagreements about the way in which the diocese and the national church used their funds. "We don't always agree with what things are done with our monies," he said, "yet you have continued to give even while sometimes disagreeing. I think this is more than commendable, I think it is <u>Christian</u>." The following year he told his people that "one of the supreme marks of a healthy parish [is] the ability of members to work together in reasonable harmony without that hideous jealousy and pettiness that rips so many organizations." A number of parishioners had expressed the desire to have Communion each Sunday at the later service as well as at the early one. "I shrink back from doing it summarily because I'm basically a coward and don't like to fight (a lover, not a fighter!), but also because I do believe in the doctrine of fairness. Many people, not only old-timers but others, have a deep affection for Matins as a service of worship. Since St. Bede's has only Eucharist at its two services, for us to adopt the same schedule would leave Matins-lovers no place to go." As a compromise he proposed to have services of Morning Prayer three Sundays in the month followed by Communion for those who wished to remain. Two years later he acknowledged the growing appreciation of the centrality of the Eucharist and said he was moving to celebrate it at the late service twice a month. There would still be Matins followed by Communion on two Sundays.

It was the senior warden, Louis Berghofer, who raised related issues in 1977. "Our parish went through a trying time," he said at the annual meeting, "following the General Convention. However I am sure this was not confined only to our parish. Regardless of how each of us may feel regarding General Convention I know that God's will will be done."[4] The fact the total annual attendance exceeded 20,000 for the first time in many years seemed to prove that the church was holding together.

Fr. Campbell's comments at the annual meeting held in January 1978, dealing with events of the preceding year, were similar. He acknowledged that attempts to assess the mood or attitude of the parish left him confused.

---

[4] Berghofer's wife was parish secretary and a strong supporter of Father Campbell.

I realize the mood on a national level during the past year has been, on the whole, rather sour because of some of the actions taken at the 1976 General Convention and on actions taken by leaders without the imprimatur of the Church generally. How much of this is localized, I just don't know. We have tried here to play it conservative, which I don't think bad. A true conservative is one who attempts to "conserve" that which is good and basic out of past experience while being open to healthy changes that bring progress.

The difficulty, of course, lies in defining "progress." Change not always is progress, despite what some people think. One of the great values of tradition in a Church like ours is that the winds of change which blow through each new generation, then peter out, do not become the new salvation. Even the church is not exempt from the temptation of being "with it" to win adherents. But, for how long are people kept who come only because of novelties? Even the most imaginative cleric has only so many new gimmicks to astound the populace. . . . We may not be as "with it" but I think we'll be around longer. I may very well be wrong. If we want guitar masses, the altar in the center of the chancel with the choir behind, the Rite 2 Eucharist (which I DO like very much) and other novel approaches, I'll be happy to try it. My point simply is this: I have tried to keep the Church as most people here seem to want it. We have not adopted novelty, not because we can't do it, but because I don't think most of the stuff going on today is long-enduring. But even more importantly, I don't think that much of it is worthy of the worship of Almighty God.

He then reverted to his quest for unity. "If we can live and let live," he said; "if we are willing in love to tolerate bores, boors, and assorted kooks; if we are willing to accept those who oppose our way of thinking and still love them; if we are willing to forgive until seventy times seven someone, be he clergyman or layman or laywoman—only then can we say we are a Christian cell worthy of the name."

Two specific issues had aroused these comments. One was the proposed Book of Common Prayer adopted at the national convention of the Episcopal Church in 1979.[5] For a time the rector was willing to continue using services

---

[5] The book was initially accepted at the triennial convention in 1976 but did not go into general use until final adoption in 1979. This writer assisted with the music at some of the services of the 1976 convention, which was held in

(1) Exterior, Church of the Holy Faith
(2) Exterior, Palen Hall

(3) Interior, Church of the Holy Faith

(4) Altar, Church of the Holy Faith. Reredos designed by Wilfred Edwards
Anthony and carved by Gustave Baumann, 1945; frontal by Phyllis
Lehmberg, 1999.
(5) The Chapel of the Good Shepherd. The carved Christus Rex above the
altar is by W. Shaw.

(6) Good Shepherd window. This stood behind the altar in the original church and is now placed on the side wall to the left of the altar.

(7) Window in nave, in memory of Hattie Estelle Childs, first wife of L. Bradford Prince, d. 1880.

(8) Window in nave, in memory of the Rev. Sanderson Henry Stefanos Ilderton, d. 1892.

(9) Window in nave depicting St. Hilda of Whitby, in memory of Charlotte Frances Trowbridge, wife of Walter S. Trowbridge, rector 1918-35.

131

*(10) Window in nave depicting St. Cecilia, in memory of Cora and Edward
L. Bartlett.*

(11) Windows above altar depicting scenes from the Creed. Designed by Judson Studios of Los Angeles and given by John Gaw Meem in memory of his father.

(12) Window depicting the Virgin Mary. Designed by Judson Studios and given in memory of Mary Vilura Conkey (1880-1963).

134

(13) Window depicting St. Francis of Assisi. Designed by Judson Studios and given in memory of Louise Beveridge Burdine (1867-1956).

(14 a, b, c) Windows in the chapel, designed by Shaw, 2001. The figures represent St. Julian of Norwich, the Virgin Mary, and St. Hugh of Lincoln.

136

(15 a, b) Processional cross by the Navajo silversmith Preston Monogye. One side is a traditional Navajo design and the other has the Christian Chi Rho monogram. Gift of Margaret and Julian Rymar.

137

(16) "Feeding the Multitude," painting in Palen Hall by M. A. Schatzie Hubbell, 1984, in memory of Virginia Lee Comer (1910-82). The kneeling figure in the foreground is a self-portrait of Mrs. Hubbell.

138

(17) Painting in Palen Hall by M. A. Schatzie Hubbell, in memory of John Gaw Meem (1894-1983). The central standing figure represents Fr. Donald Campbell.

(18) Conkey House following the addition of the second storey.
(19) The parish library.

from the 1928 Book as well as experimenting with the new Rites I and II–the old services were used on Sundays throughout 1978—but he concluded that it was contrary to Anglican tradition to have two Prayer Books and told parishioners in 1979 that he would vote against allowing continued use of the former liturgies. In 1980 he announced that he would stop using the 1928 book at the end of the year, and would also discontinue the 9 o'clock service, since it was poorly attended. He thought that "to continue longer is merely to prolong things without resolution.... The 1979 book is THE Prayer Book that sets forth the worship of our Church and I am conscience-bound to use it as our only legal book." No more than 5% of the members of Holy Faith had trouble accepting the new services, and no single member had come into the parish because of the continued use of the 1928 services. Campbell urged members of the congregation to exhibit flexibility. If begged to do so by faithful members of the parish he might still use the 1928 liturgies for weddings or funerals, but not for Sunday services.

The other divisive matter had to do with the ordination of homosexuals and women. At the annual meeting in January 1977 a parishioner (Lucy Dix) asked that those proposed for election to the vestry state their views on the ordination of women, but the discussion was tabled. The following January Dorothy Lanham, one of the most active women of the parish, moved that Holy Faith protest the ordination of "a self-acknowledged lesbian, Ellen Barrett, to the priesthood of our Church." She was "saddened and appalled" at this ordination by Paul Moore, Bishop of New York. Her motion asked that the parish's protest be registered with Bishop Trelease and Presiding Bishop John Allin as well as Bishop Moore himself and that "whatever steps are necessary to prevent legally any future ordinations of known, practicing homosexuals be taken immediately." After a number of parishioners spoke to the issue, the motion carried.

It is interesting that the stated objection was to the ordination of homosexuals, not women, as priests. There were of course many conservatives who opposed women's ordination regardless of the sexual orientation of the candidate. It had not yet been approved by the General Convention–Bishop Moore had acted on his own, without the authority of the national church. Despite his plea for flexibility on other subjects Fr. Campbell said that "as a matter of conscience he

---

Minneapolis, but did not attend the business meetings and did not realize how divisive some of the decisions would be. It is interesting to recall that many years earlier L. Bradford Prince had opposed the introduction of the 1928 Prayer Book, believing that no revision of the existing services was needed. Fr. Campbell had considered using the Services for Trial Use (the so-called "Green Book") as early as 1974.

(35) Rev. Donald L. Campbell and Rev. Michael O'Connell, photo by Louise K. Crabb, October 1979, parish archives, Box II.16.

would not allow women to preside or preach from the Holy Faith pulpit as long as he was Rector."

All in all, as senior warden Herman Barkmann said, "This past year has not been an easy one for Fr. Campbell."

There have been some local problems causing unnecessary parish division, but the greatest causes of concern for our priest have been caused by activities at both the diocesan and national level, and are actions that Fr. Campbell is dedicated to honor from his participation, as a priest, in our <u>Episcopal</u> church. It is imperative that we all realize, and make it our mission to make others realize, that withholding our support from our local parish has little effect at the Diocesan or National level. If we disapprove of actions, we must make our dissatisfaction known by letters to the Diocese or National headquarters, <u>not by penalizing Holy Faith</u>. Let us all work together for the continual unity which Fr. Campbell has returned to us at Holy Faith.

(36) Fr. Campbell receiving a bound copy of Beatrice Chauvenet's history of the parish from the author, 1978, parish archives, Box. II.16.

(37) Rt. Rev. Richard M. Trelease, Jr., photo courtesy Institute of Historical Survey.

Campbell's last years were quieter. At the annual meeting held on January 31, 1982, Martha Jones presented him with a copy of Bradford Prince's book, *Spanish Mission Churches of New Mexico*, in appreciation of his ten years of service as rector. In 1984 he thought that he had been successful in trying to "steer a middle course between old patterns and those of the new Prayer Book;" for him "the allure of the Episcopal church [was still] the dignity and refinement of its worship."

✝

Upon his retirement as diocesan bishop C. J. Kinsolving was named rector emeritus of Holy Faith. He lived in Santa Fe and occasionally preached or assisted with services. In 1985 the lounge in Conkey House was named the Kinsolving Room in his honor. His portrait was hung there and for a number of years his episcopal ring and pastoral staff, together with his cope, were displayed in a cabinet.[6]

The new bishop, Richard M. Trelease, Jr., was nominated from the floor at the diocesan convention in July 1971and elected on the seventh ballot. Father Campbell was another candidate who received considerable support; not until he withdrew on the sixth ballot did Trelease obtain a majority of the clerical votes. Trelease was the son of an Episcopal priest who had been born in Cornwall and migrated from England to the United States while still a young man. The bishop himself had been born in California but grew up in Kansas. He was ordained in 1943 and served parishes in Hawaii as well as Wilmington, Delaware, and Akron, Ohio. He and his wife Jean had two grown sons and a daughter, Phyllis, who was 15 when they moved to Albuquerque. Bishop Trelease was consecrated in Popejoy Hall at the University of New Mexico on December 13, 1971. He was to remain in office until his forced retirement in 1987.

✝

One of Donald Campbell's greatest specific needs was clerical assistance. There was just too much work for a single priest. Because of financial pressures Campbell thought that it might be possible to fill two vacancies at once by finding a priest who was a skilled musician and could serve as organist and choir director as well as curate. Harriet Heltman had relieved Mary Jean Cook as organist and choir director in 1972, but in 1973 she was replaced by the Rev. W. James

---

[6] They were removed when the building was remodeled in 2000.

(38) Father W. James Marner at the organ, from Chauvenet, Holy Faith in Santa Fe.

Marner.[7] A native of St. Louis, Marner held a degree in music and was a graduate of Seabury-Western Seminary in Evanston. He had been a church organist during his high school days and had served as rector or vicar of churches in Kansas and the dioceses of Olympia and San Joaquin; before coming to Holy Faith he was vicar of Trinity Church in Lone Pine, California. At first the budget did not include enough money for his salary, but at the 1973 annual meeting Dr. Myra Ellen Jenkins moved that the parish act with faith, hoping that each parishioner would give an additional 60 cents a week, and hire Marner. His sister came to live with him in a mobile home in Santa Fe, since Holy Faith then had no second rectory. In March the Women of the Church held a reception honoring "Father Jim" and Grace. In February 1977 Marner became ill and had to take a leave of absence. He returned briefly at the end of the year but had to retire in the Spring of 1978. He died four years later. His sister continued to live in Santa Fe and later gave the parish a bird bath in her brother's memory.

Several other priests assisted Campbell for shorter periods. The Rev. Michael O'Connell was employed as curate in 1979 but had to be dismissed a year later. His sad story has been clarified by Kathryn Campbell, who said that "he was a predatory homosexual and an alcoholic with all the evasions common in trying to hide a problem."

> At that time [Mrs. Campbell continued] I was on the staff at Santa Fe Preparatory School and heard of inappropriate advances toward one of our upper classmen. His mother was an occasional attendee at Holy Faith and another Holy Faither had suggested Fr. Mike to counsel the boy. Since I wasn't under the seal of the confessional, I confided in Don. This may have been the impetus needed in seeking professional help for Mike. At Don's (and possibly the Bishop's) insistence, he was enrolled in a treatment program in Albuquerque. Mike signed himself out of treatment and went to San Francisco for the remainder of the treatment time, but he took the precaution of giving letters to friends to be sent back to Holy Faith showing an Albuquerque postmark. He was seen in San Francisco by one of Holy Faith's gay parishioners. The letter-sending friends were mem-

---

[7] Rollie V. Heltman, Harriet's husband, was director of bands in Santa Fe; their son Gregory sometimes played the trumpet at Holy Faith and was to become the founder of the Santa Fe Symphony Orchestra and Chorus, a role he still fills with distinction.

bers of our choir and admitted their part in the farce. Don dismissed Mike the day he returned to the office.

"There is one final story," she added, "illustrating Mike's charm and glib tongue. He left Santa Fe driving a car leased from a local dealer. The dealer issued a warrant for his arrest and Mike was detained by California police to be held until the dealer's agent could arrive to make a formal complaint. Mike talked himself out of jail and was gone before the agent arrived."[8] Both Fr. Campbell and Bishop Trelease were distressed that he had lied to them about his activities.

The Rev. James Adams served far more happily from 1980 to 1982 but then left New Mexico for Wisconsin. In 2002 he was elected Bishop of Western Kansas. Adams was followed by the Rev. Kenneth Shepard (1982-85), who later worked in California. Several retired priests helped out; they included the Revs. David Tod and Charles F. Whiston. Fr. Thad Harris was at Holy Faith during the summer of 1972 while Fr. Campbell was studying at Canterbury. In 1981 Fr. Campbell exchanged pulpits with the priest of St. Margaret's parish in Buxted, England; Canon Jones took his place at Holy Faith, and his wife Betty entertained the vestry at the rectory.[9] Fr. Joachim Bakey, a priest "received" from the Roman Catholic church, also assisted in 1983 before going to serve a church in Nebraska.

†

One of Marner's concerns was the completion of the Hyde memorial organ. As we have seen, the original instrument was scaled down because of limited financial resources and a number of the stops in Ernest White's specification were omitted. Father Campbell was also eager to have the remaining stops installed, if necessary one rank at a time. In fact there had already been discussion of adding to the instrument before Marner's arrival; in 1970 Mary Jean Cook had corresponded with Dewey W. Layton, head the Layton Organ Company of Florence, Colorado (a suburb of Colorado Springs), regarding alterations. As Layton wrote, "We are certainly in agreement that the design of the organ shows a lack of understanding how an organ works as a musical instrument. One of the problems is that the organ is not really large enough to be a good three manual instrument. I could easily design a two manual organ of 30 stops which would be, in my opinion, much better than a three manual of 30 stops." He proposed add-

[8] Kathryn J. Campbell to Stanford Lehmberg, October 30, 2002.
[9] Stephen and Suzanne Watkins made their first visit to England in 1981 to visit the Campbells.

ing an 8' Principal, a 4-rank Mixture, and an 8' Trompete to the Great, a 4'
Prestant, 2' Blockfloete, and two mixtures to the Swell, an 8' Krummhorn to the
Positiv, and pedal reeds at 16' and 4' pitches. A very similar design was approved
by Marner in 1973; in addition to the changes proposed earlier it moved the
Swell Trompete to the Great and provided a new Hautbois as a solo stop on the
Swell.[10]

In January 1974 Father Campbell signed a contract with the Layton Company to make these additions at a cost of $14,560, the work to be completed
within fifteen months. The funds were to come from bequests and memorials.
Since Layton did not make his own flue pipes, they were provided by a company
in Holland. Work was completed in the Fall of 1975 and the organ was dedicated
on October 19 with a recital by Wesley Selby of the University of New Mexico,
who was also state chairman of the American Guild of Organists and organist of
St. Paul Lutheran Church in Albuquerque. His program included works by Bach,
Clerambault, and Ginastera, Liszt's Prelude and Fugue on B.A.C.H., and John
K. Paine's Concert Variations on the Star-Spangled Banner. Marner arranged a
series of recitals late in 1975 and in the Spring of 1976. Among those who per-
formed were Holy Faith's former organist Mark Davis, Geoffrey Butcher of St.
John's Cathedral, the organ builder Dewey Layton, Dr. Robert Seamon of Los
Alamos, Philip McDermott, and Marner himself. Davis was assisted by a violist,
Jan Di Janni, Marner by the pianist Gillian McHugh and, on another evening,
Herb Beenhouwer, cello. There was also a concert by the Yale-St. John's Consort,
including Scott Hankins, violin, Frank Lynch, oboe, and Manuel P. Maramba,
organ.

A number of special events took place during Marner's years at Holy Faith.
In 1974, as he wrote in his annual report, "The summer was climaxed with a very
special service of thanksgiving when the Rector and his family returned to the
parish in August [from a period of study in England]." Mrs. Campbell amplified
the situation. "Our welcome home concert was a gift from summer parishioner
Douglas Perry, a lead tenor at the Opera. He had become a friend over several
opera seasons and house-sat for us while we were in England. This worked well
for all of us; the Rectory was well cared for (as was our German Shepherd) and

---

[10] Similar suggestions were made by Eugene E. Poole, a former Möller representa-
tive who had been involved in the original design, in September 1978. Poole
added that the original instrument, which had cost $28,745, should now be
insured for $81,373. After the additions were completed the value was set at
$85,000. Correspondence, contracts, and related materials are in the parish
archives, Box I.36.

Doug had summer accommodations at no cost. Don and I arrived home on a Saturday and Doug and his thirty-two musicians took over the late service. I understand we had tourists sitting on the front steps and lined up the sidewalk. It really was a glorious day." The service included six anthems. The summer Opera apprentices were again a "real spiritual treat" in 1975, when the Holy Faith choir joined in providing music for the diocesan convention. The next year saw concerts by the St. John's College chorus and the Santa Fe Civic Chorus, directed by the church's former organist Mark Davis. There was another program by a group of Opera apprentices, and a brass choir directed by Greg Heltman assisted with music on Christmas Eve. A motet choir, newly formed to sing unaccompanied music, offered several Evensongs and a midnight Plainsong Eucharist. Bagpipers from Albuquerque were supposed to assist on St. Andrew's day, but because of a heavy snowfall their appearance had to be transferred to February 1977.

As we have seen, James Marner had to resign in the Spring of 1978. He was given a retirement gift of $500 and thanked for his five years of service. His place was taken by Daniel Kelley and his wife Sandra–he served as choir director and she played the organ until 1979, when an injury and a leg operation made it impossible for her to continue. Greg Wilcoxson was engaged as a temporary replacement and in fact stayed until 1982, but he lived in Albuquerque and was not always available when the church needed him; he was dismissed because Father Campbell had counted on him for the church's centennial celebration only to find that he had made conflicting plans. But Campbell did express his gratitude for the quality of organ music Wilcoxson had provided over the last three and a half years. Daniel Kelley remained until 1983, when Rebecca Rollett assumed the position of music director.

Despite these changes in staff the music program remained strong. In 1978 Mr. and Mrs. Daniel Sass, directors of the Northern New Mexico Children's Choir, were given permission to use space at Holy Faith for their business operations; they presented programs on November 5 and Epiphany. Mary Jean Cook and her ensemble enriched the service on Veterans' Day. Mr. Kelley noted that in 1979 the choir sang forty-one different anthems. Unaccompanied Plainsong was offered at two services (those on St. Francis' day and All Saints). Greg Wilcoxson's group called the Sun Mountain Chorale also gave a program. At the end of her first year Rebecca Rollett reported that the twenty-five members of the senior choir had sung the Schubert Mass in C as a "mini-concert." There were still soloists from the Opera and the new chorus of Santa Fe Chamber Singers gave two concerts. In addition there were Lenten programs (some of them sponsored by the Library Committee) and harp and harpsichord recitals. The junior choir had come to number only seven, but a cherub choir for younger children aged 1 to 5 had also been organized and sang "Away in a Manger" on Christmas Eve.

†

Parish statistics, set out in Appendix I below, show that the number of parishioners remained nearly constant during the Campbell years. In 1972 there were 808 baptized members and 629 communicants. The largest number of baptized members, 974, was reported in 1979, while the highest figure for communicants, 684, was listed in 1982, 1983, and 1984. (This looks suspicious, but examination of the records shows it to be correct.) In 1984 (Campbell's last full year) there were 898 baptized members; this fell to 786 in 1985. Total annual attendance figures show an increase from 17,085 in 1972 to 22,332 in 1984.

The Holy Faith operating budgets, however, rose consistently. The following table gives figures for some selected years, taken from annual reports.

Annual Budgets

Year	Budgeted Income	Pledges	Rector's Salary	To Diocese
1973	$67,500	$55,000	$9,696	$20,736
1975	83,300	71,700	12,000	24,132
1977	102,021	83,000	14,404	24,840
1981	143,300	120,000	18,000	27,769
1983	165,000	140,000	20,160	34,373
1985	189,500	161,100	23,000	42,000

It will be noted that the diocesan quota and assessment more than doubled during these years. Vestry members were not always happy about this; in one or two years the full amount was not paid, and there were attempts to discuss the Fair Share quotas.

The parish's endowments also grew rapidly. These consisted of stocks held and invested funds resulting from legacies and bequests.

Invested Funds

Year	Stocks Held	Invested Funds from Legacies
1972	$37,683	$57,279
1975	148,843	188,701
1977	208,294	215,408
1980	244,699	447,122

The Vivian Sloan Fiske Endowment, one of the largest gifts ever received by the parish, was accounted for separately. It added $148,004 to the value of legacies in 1980 and $585,529 in 1984. In 1984 the parish's total holdings were listed at $1,059,785. Vestry minutes, which include monthly financial accounts, demonstrate that Holy Faith's funds were carefully tended. Much of the credit must go to Stephen Watkins, who served as treasurer for most of these years. Walter Bruce was also concerned with financial management.

For many years the parish had used the income from bequests and legacies for special purposes, not as operating funds. As we will see, some of the revenue helped pay for improvements to the church buildings, but some was always allocated for work outside Holy Faith. During the Kinsolving years Holy Faith tithed 10% of all inheritances for the endowment of the diocese—Holy Faith and the church in Roswell basically started the endowment fund of the diocese. In 1977 Holy Faith's "tithe outside parish" (from annual income, not inheritances) amounted to $4200. During the early 1980s these grants grew to substantial proportions; applications for assistance were considered by a committee chaired for a number of years by Paul Franke. In 1983, for instance, eleven organizations received funds totaling $29,100. The largest grant was $8000 to the agency Open Hands, which provided home care and day care services for needy persons in Santa Fe. The Santa Fe Rape Crisis Center was given $5000; the New Mexico Girls' Ranch in Lamy received $5000 for provide furniture for a new dormitory; $3000 was allocated to La Familia Medical Center to cover the costs of a health educator. Although most support was given to local organizations, Holy Faith also sent $1000 to Presiding Bishop's Fund for World Relief. Grants awarded in 1984 reached a total of $40,620. Most of the same agencies were supported: the Rape Crisis Center was given $6500 toward the salary of a half-time clinician; the Girls' Ranch received $5000 to purchase a tractor to blade ice and snow; Open Hands was allocated $4000 for adult care; La Familia was given $3000 for medical services to indigents; the Presiding Bishop's Fund was awarded $1500. Among the new grants were $8000 for Visiting Nurse Services and $3300 to St.

Vincent's Hospital for urgent care.[11] As Stephen Watkins said at the annual meeting, Holy Faith was "a very solid and incredibly generous parish. Income was $4000 more than expenditures and about half of the endowment income goes outside the parish."[12]

†

Although no new buildings were erected during Campbell's ministry, a number of additions and improvements to the existing facilities were made. In 1974 a new heating system for the church and Palen Hall was installed, after years of complaints about the old one. It used hot water rather than steam. The cost was $10,000 for materials and $15,000 for labor; as the junior warden said, "All the pipes have been replaced and it should last for decades to come."

A more important addition, at least visually, was the new altar put in place to celebrate the parish's centennial in 1982. The project was under discussion as early as 1976. Originally John Gaw Meem was consulted about the altar–he and Fr. Campbell had become good friends—but his plans were never completed, partly because he favored a stone altar rather than a wooden one which would be less expensive to construct. Another advantage of a wooden altar was that it could easily be moved if the priest chose to celebrate the Eucharist facing the people–many parishes suffered bitter controversies over proposals to move historic altars in order to accommodate newer liturgical practices. In the end the altar was built to designs by Schatzie Hubbell, who was responsible for most of the art at Holy Faith during this period, and the woodworking was done by Southwest Spanish Craftsmen, a firm which was owned by her husband Richard Hubbell. The central bronze medallion representing the Agnus Dei was also designed by Mrs. Hubbell and was cast by the Shidoni Foundry. The cost was borne by contributions made by about 150 parishioners. The altar was dedicated on Friday evening, August 6, 1982, by Abbot Jon Aidan of the Franciscan house in Denver. The Abbot preached again at a special service the following Sunday, when music was provided by eight apprentices from the Santa Fe Opera.[13] As the leaflet issued at the dedication recorded, "The Holy Faith Centennial Altar project [was] originated, encouraged, and guided to completion by Father Donald L.

---

[11] Figures from annual reports.
[12] The national church also made at least one grant to a Santa Fe agency. In 1972 the vestry was consulted about an award to La Clinica and approved the allocation.
[13] There had been talk of inviting the Presiding Bishop, John Allin, to the centennial celebration, but in the end this was not done.

Campbell, Rector." It celebrates his leadership as well as the parish's centennial.

In 1976 a new processional cross given by Stephen Watkins in memory of his first wife Betty was dedicated and put into use. It was designed and made by Andrea Bacigalupa, a respected Santa Fe craftsman. The following year saw the installation of a new tower door made by Volker de la Harpe and wrought iron grilles between the tower and Palen Hall fabricated by Mr. De Leon. A wheelchair ramp was added to this area in 1978. There was talk of adding a bell to the tower, but this never advanced beyond the discussion stage. A tester was put over the pulpit in 1981, paid for as part of a bequest from Stephen Watkins' former secretary, a Canadian who had served on Lord Mountbatten's staff in Burma during World War II. In 1982 a tile mural of St. Francis made was placed on the outside wall of the church facing Palen Hall. Once again the work of Bacigalupa, this honored the memory of Lillian Rockett and was given by her sons John and Louis. A raised planter was placed in front of the art work. New stained glass windows were installed in the Conkey House hallway. Shutters made by the Southwest Spanish Craftsmen were placed on the windows in Palen Hall in the same year, replacing worn-out curtains; they cost $4358, most of which was paid by the Women's Guild rather than the vestry. Schatzie Hubbell's paintings or "frescoes" in Palen Hall were completed in 1984 and dedicated as memorials to Hazel Ham, Robert Jones, Vivian Sloan Fiske, Virginia Comer, Agnes Tait McNulty and her husband William McNulty, and John Gaw Meem. The six panels cost $9000, which was taken from bequests and memorials. Mrs. Hubbell included slightly disguised portraits of herself and Father Campbell in two of the paintings—she is the female figure kneeling in the painting of Christ feeding the multitude. Wooden figures of angels given to the church were placed on the sides of the stage at about the same time.

Throughout these years the possibility of adding a narthex at the south end of the church building, as proposed earlier by Meem, remained under discussion. The vestry minutes for September 1972 commented, "It seems we have only the plans and a lack of interest." But the matter came up again in 1981, when it was suggested that a legacy given by Hazel Ham might finance the project. The architect John McHugh said that he would like to draw up plans, presumably based on Meem's, and that the narthex might be completed in time for the centennial. A scheme for the narthex was submitted to the Historical Zoning Committee and approved in 1983, with the suggestion that trees be planted between it and Palace Avenue, but in March Dr. Myra Ellen Jenkins, the historian and archivist, came to a vestry meeting to voice her opposition. The narthex, she said, would "change the façade and character of the building"; this was particularly undesirable at a time when recent building in Santa Fe had violated the city's unique historical quality. So the scheme was dropped once again.

Finally, extensive building projects were undertaken in 1983, shortly before Fr. Campbell's retirement. These included a new priests' sacristy built at the north end of the garden, adjacent to the Altar Guild sacristy. Furnishings were provided out of the bequest by John Gaw Meem as a memorial to Mr. Meem's parents, the missionaries in Brazil. New carpeting was installed in the church and a columbarium containing sixty niches was placed in the garden. The architect for this work was Robert J. Strader and the contractor was the firm of Stearns & Dominick, which had made a bid of $52,022. The columbarium was fabricated by Armento Liturgical Arts of Buffalo, New York, at a cost of $5280.[14] In addition, a new skylight was installed in the renovated nursery room and the Palen Hall stage was enclosed for use as a conference room.

†

John Gaw Meem, who, together with his wife Faith, had done so much for Holy Faith, died on August 4, 1983. The memorial service held at the church on August 8 was an appropriate commemoration of his life and work, with eulogies by the writer and poet Peggy Pond Church, the historian Myra Ellen Jenkins, and the Provost of St. John's College, J. Burchenal Ault. A month later three nationally distinguished architects shared their remembrances at a second commemoration at the College. An obituary appeared in the New York *Times*. The architect's ashes were placed in a niche on the east side of the chancel which he had designed. A bronze plate marks the location. Mrs. Meem's ashes were added following her death in 1990. As a friend said at the time, Faith Meem appreciated that some of the offices in women's organizations should be held by younger persons, but she was always there to help if needed.

†

When Fr. Campbell came to Holy Faith there were still two active women's groups, the Women of the Church and the Guild. In their annual report for 1972 the Women of the Church said that their function was to be the "the Martha's and Mary's of the church family." They had held four luncheon meetings, one of which honored Jean Trelease, the wife of the new bishop, and five study sessions

---

[14] A file of documents related to the building project of 1983 is in the parish archives, Box I.12, together with the vestry minutes for that year.

in private homes, in addition to sponsoring potluck suppers in Lent. Attendance at meetings was about twenty. Their annual bazaar had brought in $2779, which enabled the Women to buy a refrigerator for the kitchen and new stage curtains for Palen Hall. The group no longer gave $1000 annually to the vestry, as in past years, but instead sent $1000 to a mission in Alaska. Gifts awarded in 1974 included $1800 to the diocese to fund a study of the needs in Tucumcari, undertaken as a summer project by a seminarian, and $1800 to the rector's discretionary fund. Nina Thompson became president of the Women in 1976 and was able to report that there were now meetings nearly every month. There were two rummage sales as well as the bazaar and the proceeds made possible contributions of more than $1000 for the community as well as projects at the church. Beatrice Chauvenet served as chair of the committee on community needs. Despite these successes it was decided that the Women of the Church would abandon their separate status in 1977, rejoining the Holy Faith Guild so that there would be one women's group in the parish. Jean Jennings became president of the new organization.

Although the Guild had not been responsible for the rummage sales and bazaar while the Women of the Church were in existence, it sponsored an annual silver tea (or, in 1974, a "gold coffee" at the rectory) and continued to hold monthly meetings, generally in the church parlor, with interesting programs. In 1972 these included talks by Mark Davis on the church organ, the Rev. William Crews on the Resurrection, Marion Wasson on the history of the parish library, Peggy Bruce on the book store at St. Bede's, which she ran, and John Kinsolving, who also played the guitar.

Income from the bazaar and rummage sales increased after the union of the two groups. In 1978 the bazaar yielded $3838 and the fall rummage sale $1086. About half of this was given to the parish; the other half went for community needs and for projects which the Guild had long supported, including the boys' home in Kansas. By 1981 the bazaar profits reached $6317, with rummage adding $2523; special gifts to the parish exceeded $5700. In 1983 the Guild celebrated its hundredth anniversary. It was the oldest Episcopal Guild in the state. Martha Jones was named president in 1984 and was able to report that the group had awarded a $2000 college scholarship as well as continuing its support to the church and the community. During the summer of 1985, following Fr. Campbell's resignation, the Guild held a newcomers' party, said to the first in the history of the parish. Twenty-seven newcomers attended. The rector had said earlier that the matter of welcoming visitors and new members needed attention, and a "greeters group" had been formed.

✝

The parish library continued to be one of the finest in the country, and was recognized as being such. In 1974 Marion Wasson retired after serving for many years as the head of the library committee. The vestry wished to name the library in her honor, but she declined, saying, "I have worked long and hard and lovingly to establish the name, The Parish Library, Church of the Holy Faith," and that should remain its title. Kathy Landers took over as librarian–she was paid modestly for her services, and was sent at least once to a conference of church and synagogue librarians–and Robert Waite became chairman of the library committee, followed by Beatrice Chauvenet. They led an amazingly active group of volunteers. They met each Tuesday, sponsored both talks and a series of Lenten organ recitals, prepared the altar for the Tuesday Eucharists, repaired dilapidated hymnals, held a reception in 1977 to honor Lillian Rockett's eightieth birthday and her twenty years of service to the library, and in 1979 cooked and served lunch for the Lenten Quiet Day. A special coffee hour celebrated the library's thirtieth anniversary in August 1979. The number of books in the library remained fairly constant–it was 4203 in 1973 and 4857 in 1983–but this was because a number of books were withdrawn each year as being outdated or unimportant. Yearly additions ran from 98 to 216 volumes. The collection was widely used: 578 volumes were borrowed in 1984, for example, and an additional 216 were placed on display. The value of the library was set at $14,599 in 1973 and $22,482 in 1984.

A parish book shelf, quite separate from the library, had been established in 1975 to supply and sell religious books, jewelry, and candles. It was run by Peggy Bruce, with assistance from Carol Sheffler. Its aim was to serve the parish and the community–other churches bought their candles from it–and not to make money. At the beginning it borrowed $100 from the Altar Guild (also chaired by Mrs. Bruce) to purchase an initial inventory, but this loan was repaid in 1978. By 1979 sales exceeded $1925, with a profit of $13.42. There was a loss of $381 in 1983 but a profit of $348 in 1984, when sales reached a total of $3369.

✝

Despite successes in other areas, these were not good years for Christian Education. As Appendix I shows, the number of students in the Church School declined from 147 in 1974 (this included some adults) to 49 in 1985, having seen a low point of only 39 in 1982. This was a remarkable contrast to the two or three hundred registered in the 1950s. The rector's annual report for 1978 noted a drastic drop in the Church School enrollment; he attributed this in part to the fact that a number of families with children had moved away and those who had come in were older persons without children at home. In fact the decline was not unique to Holy Faith; most parishes throughout the country had similar experiences as a result of changes in demography and the birth rate. It was the decade of the1950s, the age of the " baby-boomers," which was unusual.

Several attempts to address the matter had not been successful. When he first came to Holy Faith Fr. Campbell experimented with a 9:15 adult forum, which he said would be informal, with opportunity for discussion and questions. By 1977 this had been moved to 9:00; the rector said it was less well supported than before, perhaps because of the earlier hour. There was also a Bible study group which met at 11 o'clock on Fridays, before the noon Eucharist. These education programs for adults were abandoned in 1982. In 1973 Fr. Campbell reported that he had been attempting to get young people in grades 9-12 involved in the church. He had tried a youth choral group with guitars "to sing more of the popular religious stuff. That fell flat." The group had turned to studying love, courtship, and marriage. In 1977 the senior high school students gathered for supper on the second and fourth Sundays of each month. Young men and women from St. John's College met at the rectory every five or six weeks for dinner and a program. One of them, Victor Austin, went on to seminary and became rector of the church at Hopewell Junction, New York. He published a book of meditations and completed his Ph.D. in 2002. The Campbell's also entertained students from the College of Santa Fe. They were sponsored by Fr. Joseph LaVoie, a good friend of Don Campbell's whose mother attended Holy Faith. This group grew from five or six students to nearly forty.

In 1976 an outside Director of Religious Education, Robert Barnes, was hired experimentally for one year at a stipend of $45 a week. The vestry agreed that increased efforts in this area were needed and resolved to establish a Christian Education committee; Beatrice Chauvenet commented that "if youth found an interest in their church, more parents might be stimulated as well." But the experiment was evidently not successful; Barnes resigned in January 1977 and his departure was accepted without any comment being recorded in the vestry minutes. By 1983 the Church School director was able to report that attendance was "slowly but steadily increasing, especially among the early ages." There were 57 students in all–11 preschool, 31 in grade school, and 15 in youth groups. The older young people were renovating an upstairs room in Palen Hall for their activities. The children's choir, once so successful, now had only a few members.

One area of modest success was Camp Stoney. In 1978 it appeared that the camp might be shut down. The vestry tackled the problem in January, adopting a motion to be sent to Bishop Trelease. The members "believed Camp Stoney performs a mission outreach of incalculable value to the diocese with its work among the young people and interested adults." A committee should be formed to make it more attractive and effective; if this was not done, the property should be returned to Holy Faith, which had previously owned the land. The next month the senior warden was able to report that the resolution had been well received and that the young people had also presented a petition for continuation of the camp. In September, after the summer season had ended, it was said that the camp's need had been demonstrated and that its deficit had been cut in half.

†

As we have seen, Mary Vilura Conkey's will had provided her home should be used by Holy Faith for twenty-five years, after which the parish might sell it should it so desire. The time period expired in September 1984 and the vestry concluded that it would be wise to dispose of the property. It was expensive to maintain and might not fit the needs of all rectors and their families. In addition, it was becoming more common for rectors to be given a housing allowance so that they could purchase their own residences and thus build up equity in the properties. There was some talk of the Campbell's moving to another home, but in the end they decided they would prefer to stay in the rectory until he retired. The property was put on the market in 1985 and sold for $400,000 in May of that year. Very appropriately, the purchasers were Faith Meem and her daughter Nancy Wirth; they wished this fine example of Meem's architecture to remain in the family. It came to be lived in by Peter Wirth, the son of Nancy and her husband Dr. John Wirth, and his family. Holy Faith was able to purchase a new rectory, formerly the E. R. Wood home on Old Santa Fe Trail, for what was thought to be a very reasonable price, $175,000.[15]

In his remarks at the annual parish meeting held on January 15, 1984, Donald Campbell expressed his desire to retire in June if his health did not improve. He was suffering from emphysema—he had been a heavy smoker—and did not feel that he was able to perform all his duties as effectively as he wished. In fact he remained in office until February 1985. In his valedictory address at the parish meeting January 20, 1985, he said that "Eleven days hence Holy Faith will enter

---

[15] Stephen Watkins had suggested that Mr. Wood reduce the asking price by $25,000 as a gift to the church. He thought that was a good idea and did so.

*(39) Fr. Campbell and the Rev. Kenneth R. Shepard, January 28, 1985,
Father Campbell's last Sunday at Holy Faith, parish archives, Box II.16.*

a new era." His long tenure was unusual. "For comparison, during the thirteen years I've been in this parish, my first parish in Pittsburgh has had twelve rectors." His departure was bound to bring change, but "a truly centered-in-Christ parish will survive this change." He and his wife Kathryn planned to move to Rancho Mirage, near Palm Springs, California, which they hoped would have a "more conducive climate." They later lived in Sun City West, Arizona, and Oceanside, California, "still searching for the perfect spot," as Mrs. Campbell put it. "This was as close to perfection as we could get–four miles from the ocean and above the smog line."[16] The mayor of Santa Fe, Luis Montaño, proclaimed Campbell's last Sunday at Holy Faith to be Don Campbell Day and presented him with a special award during the service.

Father Campbell died on December 19, 1994. His life was commemorated by special services at the church he had served so well. Many parishioners remembered his sermons, which were always succinct, carefully prepared, thoughtful and rewarding. Others appreciated his success in creating a loving church in which they were eager to serve. Several sets of reminiscences published in the *Faith Way* for Epiphany 1995 provide insights into his character. Robert Culbert, a member of the choir, described a special service held in May 1984.

> Father Campbell loved good music–even church music. He did not like "heavy" organ music. His tastes were well-known to the unusually talented young woman who was the organist/choirmaster in 1984. Father Don called her "Dame Rebecca" or "Dame Becky" [Rollett]. She created a marvelous spoof Sunday leaflet for May 27, 1984, in celebration of a mythical "Feast of St. Donald The Inflexible." The prelude was by Messiaen and so was the postlude. Father Don detested Messiaen. Dame Becky listed herself as "ex-organist and choir madame." She wasn't fired, of course, for Father Don had a wonderful sense of humor. Whenever the then-Bishop, Richard Trelease, would visit Holy Faith, Father Don would introduce him to the choir assembled in Palen Hall. With a deep bow (and a poor imitation of a cockney accept) he would call the Bishop "Yer Laardship." We shall never see his like again.

Beth Noland's "Reflections of a Holy Friendship" were more serious.

> I came to know Don Campbell when, in a fit of irritation, I tried to deposit my seven-year-old son at Sunday School one morning only

---

[16] Kathryn J. Campbell to Stanford Lehmberg, October 30, 2002.

to discover that Daylight Savings had put me off and that he had missed his class and thereby become ineligible for what up to then was a prefect attendance record. At that time in the early 1970's, I did not attend any church but I believed that my son should begin receiving some Christian education. Roaming Palen Hall that morning in high dudgeon, I came upon a compact gray-haired man robed in white and exuding a fragrant cologne who asked if he could help me. I was not very gracious and the more irate I became, the more gentle and apologetic was he, whom I later learned was the rector of the parish. In fact, I think he even apologized for Daylight Savings and asked if there was anything he could do to make it up to me!

He helped her find her way into the church during a difficult time in her life. She concluded:

As with many men of short stature, Don Campbell was taller than life. Charming, feisty, reverent, irreverent, romantic, pedantic, he led Holy Faith with a velvet hammer. Your kind will not come among us again soon, dear friend.

Prior to Fr. Campbell's departure the vestry established the Campbell Trust, designed to provide him and his wife with support for the rest of their lives. Since he had never had a housing allowance he would not benefit from the sale of a home, and the pension funds administered by the national church were not very generous in those days. The trust established by Holy Faith was funded with $100,000 withdrawn from the parish's endowment. This capital was to remain in trust so long as Campbell or his wife lived and they were to receive the income from it. Upon their deaths the corpus would revert to the parish. As Campbell said, it was an unusual token of affection for his family and appreciation for his work—and perhaps for the innumerable "delicious" dinners and luncheons his wife had provided for vestry members. New candlesticks or mass lights for the high altar were given by Shaw in honor of Fr. Campbell. Another memorial was a portrait of Fr. Campbell painted by a parishioner, Ethylinda Robbins, and paid for with funds collected by Paul and Lois Franke and Mary Lou Stark. It now hangs in the Campbell Room in Conkey House. Several of those who worked with him agreed that he could be a curmudgeon, but they loved and respected him nonetheless. Although not all his efforts had been successful, he had guided the parish through difficult times and maintained the unity he so greatly desired.

10. A Time of Troubles, 1985-1995

The decade beginning in 1985 was to prove a time of troubles for Holy Faith. There were problems of leadership, of division within the parish, and of distress at changes in the national church. Some of these problems affected Episcopalians throughout the country; others seemed to be unique to Santa Fe. Donald Hathaway, the senior warden, summed up the situation in his annual report for 1986.

> I am sure [he said] that for some, this past year with its many changes has not been easy to accept. As Episcopalians we are members of an ever changing and growing Church. I would be less than honest if I said I like or agree with some of the changes, but we all have to try to understand the reasons for them and then one way or another let parish leaders know our position. We cannot oppose change by maintaining the attitude of "that's not the way we used to do it."

Upon Father Campbell's retirement the parish undertook an extensive search for his successor. There was some feeling that this could be handled by the vestry, but Bishop Trelease told the people of Holy Faith that it was better to have a separate search committee; the senior warden should not be its chairman. Elections were duly held and those chosen were Louis Berghofer, Peggy Bruce, Jack Burton, Charles Cates, Louise Crabb, Don Hathaway, Myra Ellen Jenkins, Martha Jones, and Susie Storr. The senior and junior wardens, Paul Franke and Schatzie Hubbell, also attended meetings. Mrs. Storr was named committee chair.[1] Bishop

---

[1] Primary sources for this period are the vestry minutes, Box I.13, and annual reports, Box I.5, parish archives. Records of the search committee are preserved in Box I.28.

Trelease emphasized that the parish should choose the rector. "You will select your rector, I will not! and I say again, I will not! and I say again, you will select your rector and I will not!"

One of the group's first actions was to prepare a parish profile. An elaborate questionnaire was sent to parishioners and nearly 250 responses were received. These indicated that the qualities especially desired in the new rector were spiritual leadership, the ability to conduct dignified worship services, and preaching skills. Members saw themselves as conservative and traditional, with an appreciation of the structure and orderliness of Holy Faith. They hoped their parish would remain much as it has been. Most favored the continued use of the Rite I liturgy at the 8 o'clock service but about half approved of the alternation of Rites I and II at the later service. Traditional music was generally appreciated and many welcomed the special offerings of Opera apprentices and local musicians. Pastoral care and a concern for Christian education were also important to parishioners.

Advertisements were placed in such periodicals as *The Living Church* and the clergy deployment office of the national church was asked to asked to supply information about likely candidates. By September 1985 the committee had received 106 applications, 26 of them via the national office. The committee reduced the list to ten names, then to three finalists, all of whom came for interviews in October.

Meanwhile services were conducted by an interim rector, the Rev. Jaquelin Washington, who had just retired as rector of St. Paul's Church in Lubbock, Texas, after serving there for twenty-eight years. It was understood that parish administration would be in the hands of the vestry and that Washington's work was to be liturgical and pastoral. The curate, Kenneth Shepard, left in September to assume a position in Nebraska. Father Dinegar was hired by the senior warden as an assistant to Fr. Washington but because of complaints by Bishop Trelease resigned after several months.

Several serious candidates were dropped because the search committee felt that they were too young or too fundamentalist. The committee then selected a candidate, only to have him rejected by Bishop Trelease (despite his promise that he would not interfere) as being much too conservative. It was the bishop who then proposed the appointment of Jon Simms Receconi, who already lived in the diocese and was the bishop's friend. At the insistence of the bishop he was approved by a majority of committee members and subsequently called to be rector by the vestry with the approval of the bishop.

(40) Rev. Jon Receconi, photo from Church of the Holy Faith.

Receconi came to Santa Fe from El Paso, where he was associate rector of St. Clement's Church. He had attended the University of New Mexico and General Theological Seminary in New York. He had been active at St. John's Cathedral in Albuquerque, where he had served as verger, acolyte master, vestryman, and EYC sponsor; he also had experience in the business world. His installation as rector on February 24, 1986, was attended by more than three hundred people. Bishop Trelease presided and Fr. Campbell returned as the preacher. This was the occasion on which Campbell was presented with a scroll naming him Rector Emeritus of the Church of the Holy Faith. According to the article in *Faith Way* he noticed that it mentioned his receiving the appurtenances thereof "and in his inimitable fashion quipped that he 'didn't care about the rest of it but he wanted to know what the "appurtenances" were'! Although Father Campbell's sermons are always inspiring, this one was especially eloquent and impelling. However, the solemnity of the message was lightened by typical 'Campbellisms'–the mark of Father Campbell's dry wit and humor."

The Faith Way had just come into being. On Receconi's first day in office Mary Lou Mayhew went to him to ask if he would object to her beginning a

(41) Revs. Philip Wainwright and Ralph Bethancourt blessing palms in Santa Fe Plaza, ca. 1992, parish archives, Box II.16.

monthly newsletter. She told him, "since the church has grown considerably and has three services, people don't know each other any more." She later recalled:

Father Receconi said, "Go for it," and we did. A request was made in *The Faith Way* for name suggestions, one of which was "Receconi's Rag"–fun but not what was needed–so Father R. and Mary Lou came up with the present name. *The Faith Way* has come a long way from the first issues done on a typewriter, cut and pasted and run off on a temperamental machine in the office.[2]

As the passage about Fr. Campbell shows, *Faith Way* was written with style and humor and surely did much to inform the parish and hold it together.

It was understood that Father Receconi would need the help of a curate. In March 1986 he decided to ask Philip Wainwright to come as deacon-in-training. Wainwright was born in England but had lived in the United States since 1970 except for a few years in the 1980s when he studied theology at King's College, London. He had been an assistant at the famous London church of St. Martin's-in-the-Fields. He came to New Mexico as an employment counselor at St. Martin's Hospitality Center in Albuquerque, which also served some homeless persons from Santa Fe. In addition he had worked as a deacon at St. Aidan's church in Albuquerque. Wainwright agreed to come to Holy Faith for two years, and the vestry bought a house for him near the E. J. Martínez School. He continued to work with transients as well as concerning himself with Christian education at the church. Wainwright was ordained priest at Holy Faith in February 1987 and promoted to associate rector shortly thereafter.

Jon Receconi died unexpectedly on October 15, 1987. His death was attributed to viral pneumonia, but it was later determined that he had been suffering from AIDS, and a number of parishioners recalled how thin and frail he appeared during his last weeks at the church. As the diocesan newspaper commented, "This diocese has suffered a tragic loss. Jon was one of our most promising priests; he breathed new life into the diocese's oldest parish, and he was ready to become one of the leading men of the diocese."[3] He was survived by his wife Debrot and son Ian as well as his mother and sister who lived in Albuquerque and a brother in Santa Fe. Receconi's family were well treated; they continued to

---

[2] Mary Lou Mayhew to Stanford Lehmberg, September 2002. During Fr. Campbell's years there had been a similar but more formal publication called *The Herald*. There are files of *The Herald* and *Faith Way* in the parish archives, Boxes I.43-44.

[3] *The Rio Grande Episcopalian*, November 1987.

receive his salary for six months and were allowed to live in the rectory until such time was it was needed for a successor. A memorial fund was raised, in the end amounting to nearly $3,000, and it was used to place a memorial cross (cast by the Shidoni Foundry) in the garth between the church and Palen Hall.

This time there was no elaborate search for a successor. Father Wainwright was named priest-in-charge almost immediately and soon designated rector. At the time the diocese was without a bishop; Trelease had been forced to resign because of irregularities in his personal life, including a divorce, and his successor had not yet been designated. The chairman of the Standing Committee of the Diocese, temporarily responsible for diocesan affairs, wrote the vestry that he felt the appointment inappropriate; he believed that more candidates, including those recommended by the diocese, should have been considered. The senior warden, James Spivey, responded that the parish had acted with great care and done what it judged right under the exceptional circumstances. Wainwright described himself as "an Anglo-Catholic in liturgy, a moderate conservative in theology—without, I hope, leaning towards puritanism, which is the besetting sin of contemporary conservatives, even Anglo-Catholics." In August 1988 he was married to Miss Thekla Stark, a native of California who had lived in Santa Fe since 1984 and had joined Holy Faith in 1986. She was his third wife. Her father was the California Congressman Fortney Hillman Stark, Jr.

Fr. Wainwright was instituted as eleventh rector of Holy Faith on May 24, 1988, by the interim bishop of the diocese, the Rt. Rev. William Davidson. Davidson had been bishop of Western Kansas for fourteen years and after his retirement had served as assistant bishop in Ohio. In 1988 the diocesan convention elected Terence Kelshaw as Trelease's successor. A native of northern England and an evangelical in orientation, he had been a staff member at the Trinity Episcopal School for Ministry in Pennsylvania. Several members of Holy Faith had been active in promoting his choice, in opposition to candidates proposed by such liberal parishes as St. Bede's and St. Michael and All Angels in Albuquerque, and the election was generally welcomed at Holy Faith. As the senior warden, James Spivey, noted at the annual parish meeting, "Finally, with excitement and not a little joyful surprise, we had our part in electing Terence Kelshaw as Bishop."

Wainwright set out his views in the first sermon he preached after his institution as rector. He began by stating a common conception of the parish.

> The parish of Holy Faith is a famous one. In some circles, it is
> infamous. Two years ago, when I told my friends among the Albu-

querque clergy that I was coming here, they said "you'll hate it; they're a stuck-up bunch." In the two years I've been here, as I've found myself with other clergy and in other parishes, I've heard similar prejudices expressed over and over again. "Average age about 80," I've heard a few times from people who in fact know better; and then there's the idea that we have a lot of money and don't do anything with it, neither of which is true, incidentally—you hear that a lot, and I could quote some unpleasant variations on that theme. "They haven't had a new idea since they were founded in 1868"– that's another one you hear said in one way or another by people of all kinds, even those who would like us to think they like us. "A bunch of sharks" was the description of *you* by one or two clergy who didn't think I was blood-thirsty enough to fight you—"they're only hiring you because you're inexperienced and they think they'll be able to tell you how to run the place"; I could go on for a while like this, but that will give you some idea of the kind of fame, or infamy, we enjoy in our Diocese.

Well, in fact, we deserve to be famous, but not for any of these reasons. The quotes I've been making tell you a lot about the people quoted, but they don't tell you much about this parish, contrary to popular belief–and I'll guarantee they're not telling you anything true about me, but that's another story. Well, I'm going to tell you what *is* true, *and* what is important about this parish; I'm going to tell you the real reasons why we should be famous.

Holy Faith, he said, is the Episcopal Church in a nutshell. It has people who hate the new Prayer Book and those who are eager to go beyond it in liturgical renewal. It has people who think the church should have no involvement in politics and those who believe it should have a position on every issue. "We have Bible-thumping fundamentalist evangelicals; we have speaking-in-tongues charismatics; we have ritualist Anglo-Catholics; we have gays; we have women who want to see a woman curate here, and we have women who think women should be silent in church and submissive at home." The new rector's goal was to see that the church served all these people, that none became outcasts. Despite their different views they should come and worship together, "get on their knees together in front of that altar and worship Christ together." Even if they walk away in different directions, they can learn to tolerate their differences. There is a great opportunity for learning to understand both sides of divisive issues, "to listen to each other with open minds and loving hearts, with faith that each has a word of God for the other."[4]

During Fr. Wainwright's time there was a great feeling of fellowship in the church. Mary Lou Mayhew remembered several Shrove Tuesdays when the choir and clergy, and as many others as wished to participate, presented a cabaret entertainment combined with a potluck supper. "Besides the Rolletts and Rothschilds, Wainwright himself made a big hit as a 'punk-rock' singer, with spiked hair, combat boots, a loud T-shirt and dark glasses. No one knew him. It was really fun!"

†

Finances were a problem during the ministries of Receconi and Wainwright; the endowment had to be tapped in order to maintain the programs of the parish. One can follow the melancholy story most easily in the minutes of vestry meetings.

In May 1985 it was reported that both pledge income and attendance at services were down. This was perhaps to be expected during the interim after the retirement of a long-time rector, but in August Stephen Watkins, who had served as treasurer on and off for an equally long time, said that the financial report was the most distressing he had ever had to make. It was agreed that he could take funds from the endowment if they were needed for operating expenses. In January 1986 James Spivey, who had headed the Every Member Canvas, said that the number of pledges was about the same as the year before but the total amount pledged was down.[5] The budget adopted at the annual meeting did not include a provision for a curate, and when Philip Wainwright was hired it was decided to send a letter to all parishioners asking them to reconsider and if possible increase their giving in order to provide funds for the assistant's salary. This appeal was successful: sixty-five increased pledges brought in an additional $16,000. In December it was agreed that half of the diocesan assessment should come from endowment income, the other half from pledge and plate receipts.

In January 1987 Mr. Watkins was able to report that more than half of the $12,000 deficit that existed when Receconi became rector had been gained back. It was agreed that the parish would continue its traditional tithing, giving 10% of

---

[4] The sermon was printed in the *Faith Way* for April 1988.
[5] The respective figures were $147,390 and $137,000. For details of parish budgets for the years after 1985 see Appendix 3 below.

legacies received to the diocesan endowment and 10% of the pledge and plate income to the Special Ministries fund. But the financial report given the vestry in April indicated that revenue was down and operating expenses were up. Even the Women's Guild was suffering: Mary Lou Mayhew, its president, said that the Guild could no longer pay for coffee following the Sunday services.

At the annual meeting held in January 1988 parishioners adopted a budget which anticipated a deficit of $27,666. The finance committee recommended that Holy Faith's investments should be placed in mutual funds which would yield substantially more than had been received before ($81,000 annually instead of $51,000). Despite this change the 1989 budget still anticipated a deficit–this was said to be nothing new, although the size seemed startling because of different accounting procedures, and Fr. Wainwright argued that there was nothing wrong with using the endowment to fund programs of the church. The Special Ministries committee was told that they could no longer be guaranteed any money from the endowment income, although they would continue to receive a tenth of pledge and plate revenue.

The parish budget for 1990 anticipated taking $65,000 from endowment, the maximum recommended by the endowment committee. At the annual meeting Beth Noland, the first woman to be named senior warden, characterized the proposal as a "faith" budget rather than a "deficit" one, but Mr. Watkins observed that in his experience faith never produced more than a 10% increase in pledges.[6] By August $60,000 had indeed been taken from the endowment. It was hoped that no more would be needed for the remainder of the year. As much as $90,000 from the endowment was used for operations in 1991; it was planned to take $40,000 in 1992. A letter sent to all parishioners explained the situation, stated that expenses would be cut, and asked for a 40% increase in pledges, which then amounted to an average of only $6.16 a week. There was talk of a "zero-based budget" for 1993. One of the cuts affected the parish newsletter *Faith Way*; in order to save postage it was published only every other month, and there was talk of issues appearing even less frequently. In May 1993 it was said that the increase in giving was impressive and in June it was reported that no funds had been withdrawn from the endowment so far that year, although expenses were up

---

[6] At the beginning of her term as senior warden Beth Noland was still working as an educational administrator for the state. She retired in 1990 and was able to devote more time to the church and Bible study. During the summer of 1991 she acted as director of Camp Stoney, after the bishop summarily fired the previous director.

because of the long, hard winter. By the end of the year, however, $17,000 had come from endowment funds. The figure proposed for 1994 was $19,500.

There were special reasons for some of the problems. The first involved the housing project known as St. Simeon's. Located on Cielo Azul Street adjoining the Casa Solana shopping center on West Alameda, this had been established in the 1960s by Allen Stamm as a retirement center for low-income persons.[7] The property was placed in trust and given to St. Bede's parish; when Fr. Crews, the rector of St. Bede's, moved to the church of St. Thomas of Canterbury in Albuquerque the ownership of St. Simeon's moved with him. But it was inconvenient to have an establishment in Santa Fe run by a church in Albuquerque, and in 1985 it was suggested that Holy Faith should purchase the property and manage its use. The project included sixteen rental units—eight duplexes—and was appraised at about $800,000, but Bill Rives, the Holy Faith member most interested in St. Simeon's, believed that it could be acquired for $125,000. The trust instrument specified that only a quarter of the sale price could be retained by the Albuquerque parish; the remainder would go to charity. Two of the vestry members most concerned with finance, Steve Watkins and Walter Bruce, agreed that Holy Faith should attempt to purchase the property. It was understood that Holy Faith would provide assurances that St. Simeon's would continue to fulfill the purpose for which it had been founded—the provision of low-cost housing for persons of modest means—and that it would be operated by a separate non-profit board of directors. The proposal was explained to members of the parish at the annual meeting held in January 1986.

Holy Faith did acquire St. Simeon's, duly transferring the title to a separate foundation whose members would be designated by the rector with the consent of the vestry, but the vestry minutes reveal what was called "a misunderstanding of major proportions" over the use of endowment principal to fund the purchase and the terms of repayment of its existing mortgage. St. Simeon's should have operated at a profit—monthly rents were said to be $2480 and expenses, including mortgage payments, ran only $1068. But there was deferred maintenance to consider, and several of the tenants were unable to pay their rents. Grants from the Special Ministries fund were given to some of these persons. In 1993 it was suggested that St. Simeon's should expand its services by offering assisted-living care; the vestry endorsed the concept but declined to commit any funds, although it did make a grant of $2500 for emergency repairs to the buildings. In later years

---

[7] Mr. Stamm was active in building low-cost housing in Santa Fe. He died in 2003. He was not a member of Holy Faith, although his wife Marty is.

the board of St. Simeon's did not function effectively and Holy Faith finally assumed direct control, but the project continued to pose problems.

Of greater importance was the establishment of a new mission. This had been considered as early as 1986 but postponed; in the end it was a project of Ralph Bethancourt, who had come to Holy Faith as assistant rector in 1991. In 1993 he drew up a document called "Planting a New Church: A Vision for a New Mission in Santa Fe." This said that the city continued to grow and its people had spiritual needs, but it had been thirty years since Holy Faith undertook its last mission, St. Bede's. Those living in south Santa Fe and in the suburb of El Dorado would be well served by a new Episcopal mission which could be developed by Fr. Bethancourt with appropriate supervision by Fr. Wainwright and the bishop. The style of worship, Bethancourt said, should be "purposefully distinct from Holy Faith" in order to reach the largest number of people; there would be icons, incense, crossing of oneself, and "lifting of holy hands, as St. Paul admonishes us to do." Music would range from Gregorian and Eastern Orthodox chant to renewal songs and hymns. "If we build it they will come," Bethancourt concluded.[8]

The proposal was considered by the vestry in July 1993. It was decided that for the time being the rector should discuss it with vestry members, not all members of the parish, and that something might be started in the fall. In August the vestry endorsed the concept of a new mission and agreed that Fr. Bethancourt should continue to receive his usual salary from Holy Faith while devoting half his time to the mission. Since no other assistant would be employed at Holy Faith, there would be no cost to the parish, and Fr. Wainwright said that he could manage the additional demands on his own time. By October the rector could report an "overwhelmingly positive response to the plans for the mission"; it would be known as Christ the King and would hold a Thanksgiving Day service jointly with Holy Faith before undertaking its own independent services on the first Sunday of Advent. As of January 1, 1994, Fr. Bethancourt would become an employee of the mission; his car and vicarage would be maintained by the mission out of their own funds and Holy Faith would make a contribution to the mission to cover these costs if necessary.[9] In his annual report Fr. Wainwright exulted in the success of the enterprise. "In last year's report to the parish," he said, "I asked you to make 1993 a spectacular year. You did! We did one of the

---

[8] A copy of the proposal is filed with the vestry minutes.

[9] In the end the vicarage was sold to the Bethancourts, partly because a mission could not own such property.

most exciting things we have done in long time: we sent out thirty people to found a new church, Christ the King, to serve the developing areas beyond the Interstate Highway. And we did it without ill-feeling, without division or argument."

The parishioners who transferred from Holy Faith to Christ the King included several who had been especially active at their old parish. Among these were Clarence and Patricia Rehorn and Robert and Mary Lou Mayhew: Dr. Rehorn was a former senior warden, while as junior warden Mr. Mayhew had taken a special interest in buildings and grounds and Mrs. Mayhew had edited the parish newsletter *Faith Way* as well as serving as president of the Guild. Nonetheless Fr. Wainwright was able to tell the vestry that attendance at Holy Faith was holding up and there was a "good response from people staying at Holy Faith as far as filling in the vacancies left by those going to the mission." The Every Member Canvas had been held jointly by the two groups, with the result that pledges to the parish amounted to $195,698 and to the mission $51,566. Both churches anticipated deficit budgets in 1994. For different reasons a number of persons transferred their membership to St. Bede's at about the same time; as a result the number of communicants at Holy Faith fell from 718 in 1993 to 556 in 1994.

†

Despite the rector's optimistic comments there were growing signs of dissent and division within the parish. At the annual meeting held in January 1988 it was necessary to have five ballots before the full number of parishioners had been elected to the vestry, since a 50% majority of votes, not a plurality, was required. A vocal new member said that no one who had been a parishioner for more than five years should be elected, since new blood was needed. Three ballots were needed to determine the convention delegates. Later in the year the nominating committee heard that an unofficial group was preparing an alternative list of candidates; the vestry was clear that a single list of nominees should be put forward officially. Two years earlier Schatzie Hubbell had resigned as junior warden. She said that there were "other demands on her time," but one senses some dissatisfaction and the rector said that the position should not be as "all encompassing" as she had conceived it to be. At about the same time Martha Jones resigned as chair as of the Parish Life committee, saying that the function of the committee was unclear and that it was "fractionalizing" the parish. (Fr. Receconi responded that the vestry still believed in the committee system but that Parish Life was "on uncertain ground" and should perhaps be reformed.) In 1993 Lloyd Fadrique resigned as chairman of the Every Member Canvas and raised questions about the parish's financial administration.

There was also dissatisfaction with changes in the national church. Several groups were formed to oppose its policies, especially the ordination of women and homosexuals and the mandatory use of the new Prayer Book. In April 1989 Walter and Peggy Bruce and George Blinn asked the vestry for credentials allowing them to be voting members of a Synod to be held in Fort Worth to discuss the future of the Episcopal Church. Fifteen bishops (a number of them retired) had asked for such a meeting because of their distress at actions of the national church, especially the consecration of a woman, Barbara Harris, as a bishop. It was agreed that they might go to Fort Worth but could not bind the parish. In the end two more members of Holy Faith (Tom Caton and Claire Ellen Dinelle) went to the Synod. At the annual meeting in 1991 Walter Bruce, who acted as "convenor" of those who supported the Synod, reported that there were about ninety members from Holy Faith and other supporters from Albuquerque, Taos, Los Alamos, and Raton. He described the Synod as an organization "by which traditional or orthodox Episcopalians could remain in the Episcopal Church without compromising their beliefs which have been eroded away during the past several decades;" it was firmly opposed to women's ordination, since the tradition of the church called for an all-male priesthood. Those who supported the Synod brought two speakers to Santa Fe (the Revs. Titus Oates and Peter Toon) and persuaded the rector to hold a special service using the 1928 Prayer Book. Despite these activities a survey conducted in 1991 (of which more later) found that only 2.1% of the Holy Faith parishioners were active in the Synod, and a written comment read, "I strongly disapprove of Synod activities being conducted within the context of the parish."

Another divisive action was the ordination of a practicing homosexual to the priesthood by John Spong, the controversial bishop of Newark. Bishop Kelshaw denounced this as "another self-inflicted wound in a church already bleeding to death." Two conservative national groups, the Prayer Book Society and the Committee of Concerned Episcopalians, brought charges against Spong, but they were unanimously dismissed by a panel of seven bishops appointed by Presiding Bishop Edmond Browning. Closer to home, an Albuquerque branch of the Concerned Episcopalians circulated a petition (without signatures) calling for the removal of Bishop Kelshaw. When this was brought to the attention of the vestry in June 1993 they responded that the petition "has no credibility" and affirmed their support of the bishop and his "inspired ministry."

In 1991 the vestry created a planning subcommittee which undertook a survey of opinions about a variety of issues. An eight-page questionnaire was sent to all parishioners and 142 forms were returned. The results were summarized in a report given to the vestry in June 1992. The demography was interesting: more than three-fourths of those who completed the questionnaire were over the age of 50 and nearly half were over 65. There were no college students, at least none who returned forms, and only 4.2% of the respondents were under the age of 35. The parishioners were unusually well educated; more than half had college degrees and more than a third had some graduate work. They were also generally well-off financially, with a third reporting annual incomes exceeding $50,000. Nearly 50% attended church each Sunday–half of these came at 11:00 with the other half about evenly divided between the 8:00 and 9:15 services–and 80% pledged. Views on the national church were predictably divided: 40% were undecided about its policies, 35% were opposed, and only 24% indicated support. Two-thirds of those who responded favored publication of vestry minutes; nearly all supported the music program and the appearance of Opera apprentices. Most thought that Christian Education should focus on Anglicanism and church history rather than the study of the Old and New Testaments.

Individual comments were welcomed and a number are interesting. One parishioner did not make a pledge because there were "too many liberal aspects and attitudes" in the church, but another believed that there was "an increasing intolerance of those who hold 'liberal' views." Some wanted shorter services, less singing of Psalms, and the omission of some verses of long hymns–one person thought the music chosen was "terrible and impossible to sing." It was said that the sermons "are getting duller and duller." "How about Rite II at 11:00 at least once a month," someone asked–"I am sick and tired of a constantly penitential service and would like a joyful thanksgiving Eucharist." The lack of welcome for newcomers were "so blatant it is serious"; "favored groups seem to run everything." Finally, a comment that was unusually long and strong said, "I feel the vestry not financially responsible in the last five years. Previous vestries have put the parish in debt and now the people are expected to pay for their dumbness. I won't do it. I also think the priest is overpaid and gets too many perks."[10]

---

[10] The survey instrument and the summary of responses are filed with the vestry minutes for 1992.

†

Despite these difficulties many parish groups continued their activities effectively. The music program remained strong under the leadership of Rebecca Rollett. In 1986 she reported that the size of the choirs had increased. A new adult group had been formed to sing at the 9:15 family service, and the junior choir also sang twice a month. Guest instrumentalists had included trumpeter Greg Heltman and oboist Elaine Grossman; a new choral group specializing in early music, Cantus Sacrorum Sanctae Fidei, gave a concert before the principal service on Christmas Eve. Rebecca's husband Tony made his debut as a counter-tenor in a verse anthem by Orlando Gibbons. In 1988 the Holy Faith Music Society sponsored monthly concerts by the group known as Serenata as well as performances by groups from the church itself. In addition to these events at the church there were occasional "house concerts" in parishioners' homes, and popular "choir cabarets" were held for several years. In 1989 the senior choir sang Evensong on the last Sunday of each month. Tony Rollett was employed as assistant organist in 1990–although trained as a scientist he was an Associate of the Royal College of Music in England, while his wife was an Associate of the American Guild of Organists–and began playing for choir rehearsals and some services. The music on Christmas Eve that year included Benjamin Britten's "Ceremony of Carols" with Rosalind Simpson as harpist. Several faithful singers left Holy Faith for the new mission in 1994 and the size of the senior choir fell to sixteen. Opera apprentices continued to sing at summer services, the cost of their participation being borne by Alex Abell, and there were still annual Evensongs presented by a number of apprentices and instrumentalists from the Santa Fe Opera.

There were some changes in the schedule of Sunday services. At the time of Father Campbell's retirement there were only two Eucharists, at 8 and 11 o'clock, but a 9:15 family service was added in 1986 and the time of the later service changed to 11:15. Originally the 9:15 service was short and was followed by Church School classes, but in 1989 Fr. Wainwright introduced a sermon, since he felt that the Gospel should be preached at all services. In 1991 he announced that the family service would be less formal, so that more persons might be encouraged to attend, and he said that he would consider having Morning Prayer on some Sundays. According to the annual report the Church School experienced "a definite upswing" following the arrival of a new rector in 1986. The curates–Nelson and Bethancourt–were generally responsible for the operation of the Sunday School program. In 1990 there were five classes with a total attendance ranging from twenty-five to fifty. By 1993 Fr. Bethancourt had lost interest in the education program, and in 1994 some discontented teachers complained that there was a lack of leadership. In particular they felt that they had not been consulted about the curriculum and materials to be used. Fr. Wainwright was in charge of the adult forum, which concentrated on Bible study.

The size of the youth group fluctuated; its composition was bound to change as active members graduated from high school and younger ones were brought in. In 1985 Henry Rothschild, the group's adult sponsor, reported that there were about eighteen junior and senior high school students. Later leadership was provided by the curates. For several years the young people from Holy Faith and St. Bede's once again met together twice a month. Their special activities included work days, hay rides, rafting, ski trips, lock-ins, New Year's Eve dances, and weekends at Camp Stoney. The young people also helped with parish gatherings and potluck suppers. In 1990 it was said that there was still a small but strong core group, despite a national decline of interest in young people's activities. The next year the joint meetings with St. Bede's were abandoned; there was no animosity, but interests were different. The annual report for 1994 was positive—it had been "another great year."

The Women's Guild continued its usual activities, including the Thursday morning crafts group. In 1991, for instance, the two rummage sales brought in about $4000 and the bazaar yielded $8000. These funds were used for grants to charitable organizations, improvements to the church buildings, and scholarships for college students. In that year four scholarships of $2000 each had been awarded—one went to Fr. Receconi's son Ian—and $3979 had been spent on new furniture for the church parlor and carpet for the chapel. The women were also responsible for redoing the floor in Palen Hall, a project that ran into difficulties because the contractor had not laid the subfloor properly and refused to honor his warranty. In 1988 the Guild had given $500 to the Church School, with the limitation that it should not be spent for toys. There were several attempts to organize other groups—a junior Women's Guild was tried in 1988 and a "Bethany guild" sponsored potluck suppers in 1994—but these groups did not prove permanent. The Daughters of the King also continued their work of prayer and service.

As we have seen, Holy Faith remained committed to giving a tithe of its pledge and plate income to charitable causes outside the parish. Grants were handled by the Special Ministries Committee. The amount of money available fluctuated considerably but between 1986 and 1994 it was never less than $25,000 and sometimes it was twice that.[11] Until 1992 the diocese collected 4% of each parish's annual income and forwarded it to the program budget of the National church. Because of unhappiness with some nationally supported projects this arrangement was discontinued in 1993; parishes were left free to decide themselves whether to support national programs. Holy Faith decided not to do so but transferred the 4% to its own Special Ministries budget, so that in 1993 and subsequent years it received 14% of annual income, excluding endowment interest. An increasingly large part of these funds was allocated to crisis assistance and help for independent living. Other substantial grants were made to the AIDS ministry, Open Hands, and needy residents of St. Simeon's. In 1989 $4000 was given to the building campaign at St. Bede's. Earlier $5000 had been given to the diocese's Institute of Historical Survey to assist in preparation of a history of the church in New Mexico, a project that has never come to fruition. SPCK (the Society for Promoting Christian Knowledge) also received assistance. In 1989 the vestry did not immediately allocate funds for such grants, and several members of the Special Ministries committee said that they were "greatly distressed about the non-availability of money to fund their requests." A similar concern was voiced in 1991. But in the end funds were found, even if the total budget was in deficit.

In 1987 members of the Greek Orthodox Church in Albuquerque asked if they might hold a monthly service in the chapel at Holy Faith. They were attempting to determine whether there was sufficient interest for them to organize an Orthodox parish in northern New Mexico. Fr. Receconi noted that the Episcopal Church had historically supported the Greek Orthodox Church, and the proposal was accepted. Within a few years, however, separate Orthodox churches were established in Santa Fe and El Dorado, and Orthodox believers no longer needed to use the Episcopal facilities.

No new building was undertaken at Holy Faith itself during these years, but several proposals were considered. In 1989 there was talk of constructing a parking garage. No serious plans were made; instead parking stickers were given to parishioners. Additional spaces were needed in the columbarium, and they were eventually provided, although there were delays because of financial stress. In 1993 there was considerable interest in placing a bell in the church tower. The possibility of acquiring a bell from a redundant church in England was explored and it was determined that one could indeed be found, at a cost of about $4000.

---

[11] See Appendix 3 below for the figures. In some years different documents give different totals; I have used those that seem most likely to be accurate.

A new bell could also be bought from an English foundry, or from one in Greece (this would be cheaper but less good). There was some concern that the existing tower might not be strong enough to support a heavy bell; Elizabeth Wagner, an architect who had recently come to Santa Fe from Lubbock, was asked to investigate the situation. It was suggested that the entire community might be asked to pay for the bell as a memorial to all who had died in the service of their country, with the vestry paying only $2500 out of a total cost of about $8000. The vestry "hoped to get started on something" that fall, but despite Stephen Watkins' offer to contribute $5000 nothing was done. The narthex suggested years earlier by John Gaw Meem was considered again in 1994 but the idea was dropped. Lack of funding was no doubt the main reason, although it was said that the city's historic building code would probably not permit any change in the appearance of the façade.[12] A proposal for installing loudspeakers in the church was dropped, since they were not considered necessary. The possibility of adding a second story to Conkey House, as originally planned, was raised as well. In fact it was one of the issues mentioned in the planning survey. But very few favored it— the space still did not seem to be needed—and the project was not seriously considered. What was done was to create a memorial to Donald Campbell, dedicated while he was still alive so that he might know of the parish's continuing affection. This took the form of an aumbry (a covered recess near the altar for the storage of consecrated bread and wine). Dedicated in 1990, it was designed by Schatzie Hubbell, who also provided a new credence table and a sanctuary lamp. Earlier, in 1986, Campbell had been named rector emeritus, and in 1989 Fr. Wainwright had visited him in Sun City, Arizona, where he and Mrs. Campbell were then living.

Two changes in personnel should also be noted. In 1987 Macolvio Montoya retired as sexton. He had been employed in 1952 by Fr. Kinsolving. In 1978 there had been a reception honoring his twenty-five years of service. The parish saw that he received an adequate pension and health insurance. After unsatisfactory experiments with at least two successors he was replaced by Joe Arellano, who was soon given greater responsibilities and the title property manager.

The other loss involved the parish librarian. Katherine Landers, who had devoted her life to the library for many years, died in 1991. She had returned from a trip to India on which she developed a virus; she did not see a doctor and died within a few days. This was a great shock, and the library committee was

---

[12] No doubt there would have been lengthy discussions, but the fact that a design had been made by Meem might well have satisfied the critics.

devastated. It turned out that Kathy had taken books and other materials from the library to her home. For some time the library remained in disarray, but during the summer Mary Lou Stark volunteered to take things in hand. Virtu-

(42) Maclovio Montoya (right) at reception honoring his twenty-five years as sexton, 1978, parish archives, Box II.16. On the left is the Senior Warden, Herman Barkmann.

181

ally alone she cleaned the library, which had not been cared for properly, tried to recover books which had disappeared, enlisted the help of Carol Sheffler, and established a library committee. Fr. Wainwright then appointed Mary Lou parish librarian. Since she had just retired as a first-grade teacher she was able to devote time to library. Under her quiet but effective leadership there were popular library teas, some of them honoring writers and artists from Holy Faith. She helped set up the children's library and began holding sales of books donated by parishioners in order to raise funds for new purchases. According to Kathy Landers' last count (in 1988) the library held 4522 volumes, of which 1028 had circulated during the year. The collection was valued at $25,329.

†

While attending an Evangelical conference in 1991 Fr. Wainwright experienced a religious conversion. When he returned to Santa Fe there was a general shift in his theological, liturgical, and preaching styles. He focused his ministry on preaching and teaching almost exclusively, abandoned "catholic haberdashery" for a simple surplice, and began delivering sermons lasting more than half an hour based exclusively on Biblical texts expounded verse by verse. A number of new members were attracted to Holy Faith by this emphasis on an adult conversion experience, but they had little interest in the Anglican tradition or the larger Episcopal church.[13]

Although both were conservative, Wainwright and his assistant Fr. Bethancourt grew apart because one was an Evangelical and the other a staunch Anglo-Catholic. During 1992 Wainwright also distanced himself from the lay leaders on the vestry. At the end of the vestry meeting held on May 13, 1993, one of the members, Tom Caton, "asked the vestry to pray for guidance in addressing the unrest in the parish. The vestry then discussed ways to improve communication and understanding between the vestry and the clergy." One of the problems was that the rector frequently did not attend vestry meetings. In March he had been ill. In May he was out of town for continuing education. In June he was on vacation. Wainwright seldom presided at vestry sessions. On the other hand, the senior warden, Charles McLaughlin, had been unable to attend the annual parish meeting in January, and the rector had presided.

---

[13] Several parishioners have commented on Fr. Wainwright's conversion experience, and Fr. Dale Coleman has said that he has confirmed it in conversations with Wainwright.

The matter came to a head in 1994. Wainwright presided at the July vestry meeting, though he said that his taking the chair was not a criticism of Dr. Caton, a scientist from Los Alamos who was serving as senior warden. The rector spoke about "the apparent breakdown in communication" and "what he perceived as a unhealthy spirit that is leading people away from forthrightness and certain in-nuendo when it comes to concerns about the way things are done at Holy Faith." When vestry members said that some parishioners found recent changes frus-trating, confusing, and upsetting, Wainwright apologized for any hurt that might be felt but said that he could not address any specific issues without having time to prepare a response. A majority of vestry members favored consulting Bishop Kelshaw because "the existing problem includes the imperiled relationship be-tween the rector and the parish." It was agreed that the vestry minutes were open to others and that its discussions should not be kept secret. Rob Booms, a vestryman, advocated constructive dialogue with parish members.[14]

Wainwright was informed of a special vestry meeting on September 21 but did not attend. Instead he notified members that he had written the Bishop offering to resign as of September 29, 1995. Vestry members did not believe that this date was satisfactory—it was not practical to have in residence a rector who had in fact resigned. They believed that October 3, 1994, should be his last Sun-day in office and that it would be detrimental for him to remain in the parish after that date. Wainwright did come to the regular meeting a week later. The Bishop had been invited to attend but was not available because of travel. Once again Wainwright offered to resign in 1995, but after the senior warden said that was unacceptable he offered to make October 16 his last day. "A vestry that wanted the rector out the very next Sunday must have grave cause," he said, but when he asked if anything else needed to be brought to light Mr. Booms said, "absolutely not"—there was no allegation of behavior unbecoming a minister of the Gospel. Wainwright agreed that his termination would be by mutual agreement; he did not wish to exacerbate a difficult situation. His resignation was unanimously accepted.

Almost immediately Caton also resigned his office as senior warden, saying that his scientific work made it impossible for him to devote sufficient time to

---

[14] Beth Noland's comments are interesting. "The day before I left as a deputy to General Convention at Philadelphia in 1994," she wrote, "I met with Fr. Wainwright, urging him to be forthright in his meeting with the vestry, which was scheduled for several days hence. His eyes simply hardened, and when I returned from General Convention, his days were numbered. It was very sad." (Beth Noland to Stanford Lehmberg, November 2002.)

the church.[15] Mr. Booms succeeded him. The vestry agreed to a severance agreement suggested by the Bishop. This provided that Wainwright should receive a full year's salary as well as pension and insurance payments and that his family might continue to live in the rectory for a maximum of three months. Copies of the agreement were posted in Palen Hall so that parishioners might read it. Within a few months the former rector and his family moved to Falls Church, Virginia. He later served as rector of St. Peter's Church in Pittsburgh.

It was only natural that parishioners would react to these unusual events in different ways. Several expressed their views to the vestry. One parishioner believed that they had been duped by the Devil. Another expressed appreciation for Wainwright's orthodox beliefs and inspirational preaching. One woman wrote that Wainwright had ministered to her effectively during a period of suffering; she would be lost without him. On the other side, a couple who had been active at Holy Faith for years wrote Bishop Kelshaw reiterating their unhappiness with the rector, which they had expressed in earlier letters to the Bishop and consultations with the vestry. They added that the vestry had been properly elected and had acted appropriately.[16] A handful of people expressed their discontent by transferring their membership to the mission of Christ the King.

A pastoral letter from Bishop Kelshaw to members of the parish expressed the hope that they would avoid the temptation to "hurl vocal grenades" or engage in intrigue and rumor, no matter how badly they felt hurt. He had invited the Rev. Ivan Weiser, who had come to New Mexico from Epiphany Church in Tempe, Arizona, to serve Holy Faith as interim rector. Weiser had studied history and theology at the University of Chicago, the University of Toronto, and Oxford and had been a member of the staff at St. Thomas Church in New York City for seventeen years. He would be assisted by Fr. Dinegar in his liturgical and spiritual duties, while the vestry would manage parish affairs until a new rector could be named. The vestry might appoint members of a search committee or act as such a committee themselves; there was no single acceptable way to proceed. In any case the Bishop should be kept informed of any list of final candidates. If there was a point of consensus, it lay in the hope that the search committee would find a candidate who could reunite the church and end its decade of division.

---

[15] Dr. Caton was a friend of Fr. Dinegar, who regarded him as "a fine Christian gentleman" (Dinegar to Lehmberg, November 2002). Following the events at Holy Faith, which he said he regarded as "the most un-Christian thing I've ever seen," he converted to the Roman Catholic church or, as he put it, "crossed the Tiber to Rome."

[16] This correspondence is filed with the vestry minutes.

11. A Phoenix Arising, 1995-2000

At the annual meeting held January 29, 1995, senior warden Rob Booms said that he had found the parishioners of Holy Faith "supportive and full of Christian charity." They were "ready to begin the all-important process of finding a new rector. This will require of us a willingness to elevate the best interests of the parish over any particular theological agenda." Bishop Kelshaw, who was present, explained the search process. A search committee should give the bishop fifteen to twenty names of candidates; he would screen them and exercise his right of deciding whether they would be permitted to come to his diocese. The finalists might visit Santa Fe. Subsequently the search committee would recommend a candidate, who would be elected by the vestry and approved by the bishop.[1]

The large search committee named by the vestry included George Blinn, Mary Alice Bohle, Peggy Day, Jon Indall, Virginia Leidler, Allen Mason, Henry Rothschild, Rickie Sherrill, and Richard Simpson, with Lee Ice and Rosalind Plank as co-chairs.[2] They had been chosen with an eye to diversity in age and opinion, but according to their later report they soon became "a close and harmonious group." They worked from a list of eighty-some candidates. After studying taped sermons and service leaflets the committee selected a number whose parishes were visited by committee members. Finally five finalists were designated and in January 1996 recommended to the vestry. According to the report any of them would have been well suited to the position.

---

[1] The primary sources for this period are the annual parish reports, Box I.6, and the vestry minutes, Box I.15, parish archives.

[2] Roz Plank moved away from Santa Fe during the earlier stages of the committee's work so the burden of work fell upon Lee Ice.

One of the finalists withdrew from consideration because a family member had medical needs that could not be cared for properly in Santa Fe. The remaining four visited Holy Faith during February and March, preaching and meeting with parish leaders. There was "full and frank discussion" at a special meeting of the vestry held on March 25. Their initial vote was divided five to four, but on a second ballot the vestry voted unanimously to call the Rev. Dale Coleman, subject to approval by the bishop. Shortly thereafter, on Maundy Thursday, Fr. Coleman wrote that he was delighted to accept and "filled with a sense of indescribable joy." He would begin his ministry on June 15, 1996.

Born in Michigan, Fr. Coleman had studied at the University of Wisconsin and at Nashota House, a small traditional seminary in Wisconsin. Both of his parents had been officers in the Salvation Army, but while in college he had been drawn to the Episcopal Church. His most recent appointment was as rector of St. Matthias' Church in Shreveport, Louisiana. He had edited a posthumously published book, *The Anglican Spirit*, by the hundredth Archbishop of Canterbury, Arthur Michael Ramsey, whom he had known at Nashota House. Published by Cowley Press in 1991, the volume which describes the Anglican heritage sold over 10,000 copies, the most at that time for the Episcopal Book Club.

Fr. Coleman was soon named an honorary canon of the diocese, as Donald Campbell had been. He, his wife Sue, and their daughters Jacquelyn and Gillian moved into a new rectory on Passaje del Herrero in south Santa Fe, chosen by the Coleman's after visiting several possible houses and purchased by the parish for about $350,000. After presiding at well-attended Easter services Fr. Weiser left his position as interim rector. It had been suggested that he remain as an assistant ministering especially to older parishioners, many of whom had come to regard him highly, but this possibility did not materialize. He and his wife Toni were presented a pot made by the famous potters Maria and Julian Martínez as a farewell gift. They wrote that it was of museum quality and greatly appreciated. They continued to live in Santa Fe.

One of Coleman's first acts was to hire Phyllis Orbaugh as Coordinator of Ministries. Born in Illinois but brought up in Tulsa, she had held a similar office at the rector's former church in Louisiana; she was soon to assume responsibilities for Christian education and crisis assistance as well as securing volunteers for the various parish programs. Coleman asked Robert Dinegar, who had submitted his resignation when the new rector was appointed, to remain as an associate priest. Continuity was also provided by Suzanne Spivey, who remained as parish administrator, and Joan Garcia, parish secretary. Coleman later said that his chief support during his earlier years came from Pat and Suzanne Spivey, Noel and Lee Ice, Steve and Suzanne Watkins, and Richard and Jetta Simpson.

Shortly before Colemans' arrival there had been problems with the music department. Anthony Rollett been dismissed by Fr. Weiser in 1995 and Rebecca Rollett resigned, leaving the positions of organist and director of music vacant. After a short time serving another church the Rolletts moved from Santa Fe to Pittsburgh, where Tony was employed by Carnegie Mellon University as a metallurgist. (While in New Mexico he had been a scientist at Los Alamos as well as a musician in Santa Fe.) Richard Stark, a long-time parishioner and musician-in-residence at St. John's College, was then asked by the vestry to "help out for a couple of Sundays." His musical training and experience had been extensive, beginning as a choir boy at Grace Episcopal Church in Colorado Springs, ma-

(43) Rev. Canon Dale Coleman and Rev. Dr. Robert Dinegar, photograph by Harry Orbaugh.

joring in music at Colorado College, earning both a bachelor's and master's degree in music at Yale University's School of Music, and having years of choral conducting and music teaching experience. His initial months were difficult, since virtually the entire choir had left along with the Rolletts, but he was able to lay the foundation for a successful music program. He later commented that his thirty-month "couple of Sundays" was a great experience and that he had enjoyed working with three indispensable people—Susan Sommers and Grant Macdonald as a small music committee and Ivan Weiser as interim priest. He was succeeded by Dianne Brehmer Bailey as organist and David Arellanes as choir director. Arellanes was also director of the Pro Coro concert choir and brought several singers from that organization with him; he was a fine tenor soloist himself. In 1998 J. Michael Case was employed as organist, replacing Dianne Bailey, who had taken a position in Albuquerque. A native of Brevard, North Carolina, Case had a degree in organ performance from the University of Indiana and had served churches in Dallas and Denver; he came to Holy Faith from a position at St. Bede's. Arellanes retired in 2000 because of ill health and was replaced as music director by Gerald Near. Born in St. Paul, Minnesota, in 1942, Near had studied composition in Chicago with Leo Sowerby and conducting at the University of Michigan. For several years he had served as canon precentor of St. Matthew's cathedral in Dallas. He was a well-known composer, several of whose hymn tunes had been included in the 1982 Hymnal.

†

A parish profile issued in July 1995 described the parish's goals. First, it said, it was necessary to attract more young people. But the parish also needed to achieve "a rapprochement between those who are unwilling to accept change and those who want to change everything." Perhaps achievement of the latter would lead to the former. The rector intended to offer "medium high church liturgies," preferring the Rite I Eucharist. He perceived that there was still a latent divisiveness in the parish—the fact that no candidate for the vestry in 1995 had been elected on the first ballot perhaps proved the truth of that view—and, like Fr. Campbell earlier, he viewed his own mission as one of unification. "After ten years of conflict," he told the vestry in 1997, "the parish could expect three or four more years of difficulties before all problems are ironed out." He undertook an active program of visiting parishioners' homes and holding adult forums to discuss the state of the church. He believed that a Journey in Faith program lasting for nine months, led by both clergy and lay people, was important in preparing older young people and adults for mature Christian faith before they were presented for baptism (if not already baptized) and confirmation.

Early signs were encouraging. In his annual report for 1997 the rector was able to say that attendance had increase by nearly 20%; "a reverent and joyful time of worship has attracted many newcomers, along with many who have returned to their church home."[3] Holy Faith had succeeded in turning around a five-year decline in membership and attendance. Finances improved as well. Ann Brennand and Richard Simpson, co-chairs of the Every Member Canvas, announced that pledges were up by 30%–"this is almost unheard of," they said at the annual meeting. Operating expenses had risen only 2%. It had still been necessary to take $66,000 from investment income for parish operations during the previous year, but this was less than the average of $87,000 a year withdrawn during the previous decade. Molly and Jack Lott provided strong leadership for several stewardship campaigns, in one of which the average weekly giving of those who made pledges nearly doubled, rising from $25 to $46.

Conservative attitudes, however, continued to be strong. As Coleman said, "our parish remains traditional, with many Synod members as parishioners." A resolution stating that no action of the General Convention "contrary to Scripture and Apostolic teaching of the church shall be of any force or effect in this diocese" was passed at the Holy Faith annual meeting in 1997. Proposed by Walter Bruce, leader of the Synod, and supported by Fr. Coleman, it was motivated by objection to the national church's policy that women priests should be accepted in all dioceses, to the ordination of homosexuals, and to the use of inclusive language in the Book of Common Prayer and new translations of the Bible. But the diocesan committee on constitution and canons chaired by Patricia J. Turner, chancellor of the diocese and a former leader at Holy Faith, decided to recommend that the resolution not be passed by the diocesan convention, and it was not. Holy Faith also declined to host a conference on human sexuality, as proposed by Beth Noland, and it welcomed visits by Jack Iker, bishop of Fort Worth and a leader in the Synod, and James M. Stanton, bishop of Dallas and president of the American Anglican Council, described by Coleman as "a leader among the Bible believing bishops in the Episcopal Church." Bishop Kelshaw encouraged parishes to affiliate with the American Anglican Council and hoped that individuals would become members and contribute to the cause. At a special

---

[3] Statistics showed that six persons had transferred their memberships from St. Bede's to Holy Faith, thirteen from Christ the King. But four Holy Faith parishioners had gone to St. Bede's and eleven to the mission.

(44) Rt. Rev. Terence Kelshaw, photo courtesy Institute of Historical Survey.

(45) The Rev. Deacons Joan Garcia, Beth Reynolds Noland, and Phyllis Orbaugh, photograph by Harry Orbaugh.

parish meeting Holy Faith voted to endorse the theological position of the Council but not actually to join the organization. Fr. Coleman's own position was different from that of the lay leaders whom he found entrenched on his arrival. He had always been a supporter of women's ordination—with a mother who was an ordained Salvation Army minister, how could he not be?—and he invited several women to preach from his pulpit. The Very Rev. Peggy Patterson, dean of the cathedral in Wilmington, Delaware, was the first woman priest to celebrate the Eucharist at Holy Faith in June 2000. The first women to be ordained at Holy Faith were Beth Noland and Phyllis Orbaugh, who were made deacons in July 2001. They were the first women to be ordained in the diocese. The following year saw the diaconal ordination of Joan Garcia. All were important in the life of the parish. Joan served as parish administrator with rare efficiency and courtesy, while Beth was active in leading Bible study groups. Phyllis continued to direct Christian education and volunteer activities. Earlier, during Fr. Receconi's ministry, two men from Holy Faith, Bill Rives and Dick Tolen, had been ordained deacons and had served the church.

†

A number of changes and improvements in the church's physical facilities were made shortly after Fr. Coleman's arrival. In 1996 the altar was pulled out from the wall, so that a priest celebrating Communion might stand behind it and face the congregation. Such a change was common throughout the church at the time; Fr. Coleman had no objection to it and fortunately the Holy Faith building was able to accommodate it without any significant alteration. Comparable changes in other churches, especially those with historic buildings, often proved controversial. A chair to commemorate the service and final resting place of Fr. Campbell was commissioned as a gift from Frank and Andy Thornton and placed to the left of the altar. A new font designed by Jeremy Morelli was installed in memory of Nan Jones, and new carpet for the church was given by W. L. Button in memory of his wife. Two of the existing stained glass windows in the nave received new dedications. One now commemorated the contributions of the Holy Faith Guild and the other honored the memory of Mary Florence Langworthy, who had recently left a significant bequest to the church. In 1999 beautifully carved new front doors were installed in the church as gift from Dick Jones. New sets of blue and white vestments and appointments were designed and executed by Phyllis Lehmberg, whose ecclesiastical needlework graced churches and cathedrals throughout the country. Improvements were made in the chapel and a Christus

Rex sculpture by Shaw was placed above the altar, the previous Good Shepherd being moved to the rear of the room. The offer of an electronic organ for the chapel was rejected–the appointments committee thought that a small pipe organ would be more pleasing aesthetically–as was a suggestion that Stations of the Cross be installed. The possibility of procuring a bell from England was once again discussed, since Steve Watkins had offered to pay for it, but it was said that the tower would need a superstructure to support a swinging bell so as before nothing was done. (The bell could of course have remained stationary and been struck.)

More important was the renovation and expansion of the church's pipe organ. This had been under discussion before Fr. Wainwright and Rebecca Rollett left, but nothing definite was done until the beginning of Michael Case's tenure as organist. In January 1999 the church signed a contract with Wilson Associates of Colorado Springs, who had been maintaining the organ for a number of years, to add eleven new stops, rearrange and revoice some existing ones, and modernize the console with an electronic system of combination pistons. Several new stops went into the Positiv manual. A Festival Trumpet was made playable at three different pitches and from all three keyboards. Perhaps most important were the seven new pedal stops, including a 32' Untersatz and a 32' reed. Made by the Walker company, these were electronic rather than pipes–there would have been no room for such large pipes in the church, and they would have been very expensive. The total cost of the work was $127,900. It was completed in 2000. Several large contributions and a number of smaller ones were received, and the remaining cost was taken from investment interest. The resulting instrument is certainly the finest in Santa Fe and probably in all of Northern New Mexico; if it has a fault, it is that the voicing may be too loud and shrill for the relatively small building in which it stands.[4]

†

A long-range planning committee was established in 1997. It had fifteen members and was chaired by Rob Booms. Among the materials its members studied was a pamphlet by Arlin J. Rothauge called "Sizing up a Congregation for New Member Ministry," published by the Domestic and Foreign Missionary Society. This suggested that there were four stages of church growth: the family church, with an average Sunday attendance of fewer than 50; the pastoral church, with a congregation of 50 to 150; the program church, serving 150-350 people;

---

[4] The contract and correspondence are filed in Box I.36, parish archives.

and the corporate church, an "extra large church" with more than 350 members attending. Average Sunday attendance, not the number of baptized persons or communicants, was what counted. By this criterion Holy Faith had been a program church for some years; between 1991 and 1999 its average attendance had fluctuated from a high of 285 in 1991 to a low of 213 in 1995 and a new high of 324 in 1999. In churches of this sort it was natural for many members to miss the sense of personal pastoral care that a small church might provide, and it was inevitable that not all members would know each other or appreciate their points of view; on the other hand such a church was large enough to provide a variety of programs serving specific groups within the congregation. Holy Faith might soon become a corporate church—in fact according to this analysis it did so in 2000 when the average Sunday attendance reached 362. At this stage, Rothauge wrote, "There is a sense of belonging to something awesome when the community gathers in worship; the head priest is seen as presiding over a massive family. Much of the pride and loyalty in the congregation comes from being part of the majesty that is created by the large proportions of the church, the numbers, and the authority of the visible leadership. Newcomers might be attracted by an impressive worship service, powerful preaching, or a grand building." But corporate churches could not rest on their laurels; it was a major responsibility of a corporate church to help provide for missions in new population centers, for the chief way in which the church could grow was through the establishment of new family churches.[5]

Holy Faith wrestled with these issues in various ways. The long-range planning committee felt that it might be necessary to go to three services on Sunday mornings in order to avoid over-crowding at 10:30. Meanwhile regular attenders might be encouraged to sit toward the front of the nave or in vacant seats in the choir. There was inadequate space for Sunday School classes as well—a temporary expedient might be the use of rooms at La Posada, the inn across the street from the church, but a more permanent solution would be the addition of a second storey to Conkey House, as had originally been planned. The role of the mission of Christ the King and the possibility of greater cooperation with St. Bede's parish were also to be considered.

The final report of the planning committee was indecisive and understated. The church should certainly not consider moving to a new location where more

---

[5] This pamphlet, together with several other studies and the papers of the long-range planning committee, are with the Parish Papers and Documents in Box I.24, parish archives.

space might be available; "Holy Faith should stay where it is and prepare for modest growth. We should stress our distinct style as we are not really competing with other Episcopal churches in the area." Members should realize that they belonged to a program church where the rector could not do everything: "lay leadership has to share the workload."

Initially Fr. Coleman opposed a third Sunday service; without assistance he simply could not undertake it. In 1998 it was suggested that the later service should be moved from 10:30 to 11:00, so that there would be more time for Church School classes, and the possibility of having hymns and organ music at 8:00 was discussed. The annual report for 1999 admitted that the church was "crammed to the rafters" at the 10:30 service, since attendance had increased 40% in two and a half years. The question of adding a third service or encouraging attendance at the mission was discussed at the May vestry meeting. In the Fall of 1999 the third service was finally introduced. By this time the Rev. Logan Craft had joined the staff as curate, so that Fr. Coleman could count on assistance with the later services. Fr. Dinegar continued to be chief celebrant at the early service. This Eucharist was moved from 8:00 to 7:30 so that the next service could begin at 9:00, and the late service was changed from 10:30 to 11:15. The 9:00 and 11:15 services would be identical, with music at both; a small vocal ensemble of section leaders would sing at 9:00 with the full choir at 11:15. By April 2000 the Church School had found that this schedule did not provide enough time for classes between the 9:00 and 11:15 services, so in June the late service was rescheduled for 11:30. Obviously there were some disadvantages. Music expenses naturally rose, and those who came regularly to one of the services had little opportunity to meet those who attended another. But with a relatively small historic building which could not be expanded there were really no alternatives. And, as we have seen, Holy Faith had offered three Sunday services on earlier occasions, the difference being that the middle one had formerly been a family service closely related to the Church School rather than being identical to the late liturgy. Even the new services were often crowded. In August 2000 the average Sunday attendance rose to 400 for the first time.

In addition to the regular services on Sunday morning Holy Faith began to offer a fuller range of Anglican liturgies. The traditional Holy Week and Easter services which Fr. Coleman introduced in 1997 were especially meaningful for many parishioners. These included the full Easter Vigil and the first Eucharist of Easter. There were also special services at Christmas, including the pageant which had been greatly loved for so many years.

†

The prospect of providing additional space for offices and classrooms was more daunting. At the annual meeting in January 1999 the junior warden, Mike Ward, said that the vestry was considering the possibility of adding a second floor to Conkey House. They began working with Chris Larsen, a member of the architectural firm Dekker/Perich/Sabatini in Albuquerque. It was realized that the existing structure would have to be brought up to code and would be unusable during construction. Possibly, the consultant thought, it would be better simply to demolish Conkey House and start from scratch.

It was soon decided, however, to proceed with plans to expand Conkey House and also renovate Palen Hall. For some time the church had been inquiring whether any adjacent buildings might be for purchased. Just when it was needed a small B & B on Paseo de Peralta, the Inn of the Animal Tracks, became available. It was purchased for about $500,000 and was remodeled so that it could accommodate the parish offices while Conkey House was unavailable. The architects estimated the total cost of the building project at two million dollars. After lengthy discussion the vestry voted in January 2000 to go ahead. A building committee was named; it was to be chaired by Walt Sommer, with Nan Dieterich, Janet Kaye, Pat Spivey, Richard Simpson, Molly Lott, Joan Garcia, and Mary Bush as members. Liaison with the vestry was assured by the appointment of Molly Lott as senior warden and Nan Dieterich as junior warden.

A feasibility study showed that it should be possible to conduct a capital funds drive for $2.5 million. Arrangements were made for a bank loan which would cover expenses until the special contributions were received. In June 2000 parish offices moved to the former Inn of the Animal Tracks; at Steve Watkins' suggestion it was now to be called Faith House, the name that had been used for the earlier classroom building behind the church. Jack and Molly Lott and Jane VanderVelde and her husband Roger Walsh agreed to serve as co-chairs of the capital campaign committee. After representatives of several construction firms were interviewed the Jaynes company was chosen as general contractor. Talks with the Historic Review Board concerning the addition to Conkey House were initiated and permission to proceed was granted with surprisingly little difficulty; as the committee noted, the second storey could hardly be seen from the street, and that fact that it had earlier been blessed by John Gaw Meem must have eased the way.

By September the so-called "quiet phase" of the campaign had raised more than $668,000. After a broader appeal that had grown to $1,265,875 by the end of the year. At the annual meeting in January 2001 it was reported that Faith Works, the name adopted for the project, was only $78,000 short of its $2.5 million goal. Construction was supervised by Walt Sommers and, after he retired from his position at Los Alamos and began spending less time in Santa Fe, by Richard Simpson. As work progressed it was discovered that some additional problems needed to be addressed, so that in the end the total cost amounted to about $3.2 million. By the end of the year it was all done. Fr. Coleman was able to describe the achievement in his rector's report to the annual meeting in January 2002:

> We, together in God, completed our enormous building projects, both the renovation of Palen Hall and surrounding area and the remodeling and addition to Conkey House. In Palen Hall this was the first serious repair and re-working of this historic property in as long as seventy years! Wiring was re-done, new bathrooms suitable for a modern church were built, asbestos removed, a kitchen with ceiling and shelving dating back to the Great Depression gutted and replaced, ramps and a new heating system installed–all this just in Palen Hall. With Conkey House, we discovered an inadequately girded building from the 60's which had to be strengthened before remodeling and adding to the first floor, and then adding a second floor to this necessary office and classroom structure. With the addition of Faith House, we have offices, meeting rooms, classrooms, nurseries of beauty and grace appropriate to God's people! And with the new parking lot, we can feel proud of what we have accomplished and will be used by so many for generations to come. This is the finest and most challenging work Holy Faith has ever attempted, and which we have now completed.

New furniture for the offices and classrooms was provided, and the buildings proved both serviceable and beautiful.

†

The new facilities made possible an expended Church School program, ably administered by Phyllis Orbaugh. Members attending the annual parish meeting in January 1999 were told that the attendance at Sunday School classes had tripled in the last three years, and it continued to rise. During the sermon time at the later services a number of younger children went to Kids' Church, where they held their own worship services under the leadership of Leta Lanier, an expert in Montessori techniques. More effective work with high school students was instituted by Fr. Craft; when he found himself happier working with young adults rather than students it was carried on by a new youth minister, Brent Harvey. Joan Garcia assisted with the youth program and oversaw the work of the acolytes in addition to running the parish office with exemplary efficiency. Every summer about a dozen young people from Holy Faith attended Camp Stoney with scholarships provided by the parish. In the summer of 1999 a number of young persons from Holy Faith joined a pilgrimage to the Holy Land led by Bishop Kelshaw; again the parish paid their expenses. Adult education held between the two principal Sunday services included a Bible study group as well as the Rector's forum, which also examined a portion of the Bible, for example the book of Genesis, each year. Weekday Bible study groups were also formed, led by Fr. Craft and Deacon Beth Noland. For several summers Stanford Lehmberg took over the adult forum and offered studies of the English Reformation and English cathedrals, subjects on which he had written extensively. He also led a tour of English cathedrals in the Fall of 2001. Other lay men and women led Bible study and prayer groups, a Rosary Society, and a chapter of the Order of St. Luke which emphasized a healing ministry.

The outreach activities of Holy Faith remained remarkable. One of Fr. Coleman's first actions, reported to the parish at the 1997 annual meeting, was to expand the responsibilities of the Outreach Committee so that it dealt with grants, taking over the work earlier handled as Special Ministries. Since the parish was still not contributing the 4% earlier given to the national church, that amount was added to the usual tithe of pledge and plate income so that the committee could distribute 14% of this revenue. In addition, it was still thought that at least some of the endowment income should be used for projects other than usual operating expenses. In 1997 the committee allocated about $15,000 for work in Santa Fe, $10,000 for activities within the diocese, and $12,000 for worldwide missions. Local organizations receiving assistance included Open Hands, the Rape Crisis Center, St. Elizabeth's Shelter, the Salvation Army, and the Hospice Center. Camp Stoney was given $3000 to purchase a new computer. A church in Grand Forks, North Dakota, was sent $4000 to repair severe flood damage. International grants included substantial gifts to the South American Missionary Society, the diocese of Chile, work in Central and South Africa, schools for homeless boys and girls in Honduras (El Hogar and Our Little Roses), Russian ministries, and the SPCK. In several cases there was personal as well as financial involvement. Betsy Hake, a medical missionary, represented the church in Honduras. Mike and Alexandra Ward visited Chile, a companion diocese, and delivered the check from Holy Faith, while Don and Gene Pattison were involved in missions to Russia. During his earlier years Fr. Coleman himself handled crisis grants, assisting twenty persons or families in need with funds totaling nearly $3000. Nashota House, the rector's seminary, was generally given about 1% of pledge and plate income, as suggested by diocesan guidelines.

Besides sending funds to St. Elizabeth's Shelter, Holy Faith had a group of volunteers who prepared a complete dinner for thirty-five homeless persons at the shelter once a month. This work was led by Peggy Day and Janet Kaye. In 1998 $2500 was given to the Pro Coro Youth Choir directed by David Arellanes, with the suggestion that the group might present a program at the church. Two years later a Pro Coro trip to Mexico, intended partly to support an orphanage, received $5000. In later years a larger proportion of Outreach funds were used for programs at Holy Faith itself. After his appointment as music director Gerald Near broadened the music program and established a series of concerts by a Holy Faith chamber orchestra and the professional singers known as the Camerata; this was regarded as an Outreach activity since it brought a number of new people into the church. Near was also commissioned to compose an organ concerto and some other works for the church. The program of crisis grants expanded enormously. Investigation of the actual circumstances of those in need who came to the church for assistance was an impossible task for the rector. It was handled for several years by Deacon Phyllis Orbaugh, and finally Holy Faith recognized the necessity to employing a knowledgeable specialist in such ministry, Meredith Lowry. As Noel Ice, the parish treasurer, told the vestry in the year 2000, the Outreach Committee might well allocate a greater proportion of its funds to crisis assistance, "since Holy Faith actually does a more efficient job of helping people in financial need than some of the local organizations that the Committee helps fund." Darlene Haskin served as committee chair during this period of expanded and reassessed activities.

The Women's Guild also continued its charitable activities. Until its work was disrupted by the remodeling of Palen Hall the Guild still held two rummage sales a year as well as the annual St. Nicholas Bazaar. Revenues from these enterprises provided college scholarships for students from the diocese, uniforms for the mariachi band at Kaune elementary school, and children's books for the Santa Fe Public Library. A Community Needs Fund of $2000 was divided among other community organizations, including Alvord school, Church Women United,

La Luz Shelter, Amigos del Valle, and the Bienvenidos shelter for homeless men. Since several women from Christ the King mission were members of the craft group at Holy Faith, the Guild donated a quarter of its income to the work of the mission. The Guild also made annual contributions to the Holy Faith Altar Guild and the Daughters of the King.

The vestry informed the Guild that it would be impossible to hold rummage sales during the year of construction and that they should not be resumed when the work was complete. Storage of items for the sales, it was said, took up too much room, and the sales were disruptive for staff members and other users of the church's facilities. The loss of the sales naturally reduced the Guild's revenue, and many poorer members of the Santa Fe community lost an opportunity to acquire good clothing at modest prices. To compensate for the lost income, the vestry gave the Guild authority to allocate $3200 or $4000 a year in Outreach funds for several years. This arrangement, however, did not become permanent. Monthly programs were also abandoned at the end of the century. The bazaar, however, continued to be held early in December each year, as it had been for a more than a century–in 2000 the bazaar celebrated its 117th anniversary. In addition to providing an opportunity for many people to find unusual hand-made Christmas gifts, it was always a social occasion, with lunch and refreshments served. Leadership for the Guild was provided by Virginia Leidler, Martha Jones, Jane Amos, and Phyllis Lehmberg.

Holy Faith also provided assistance to a number of low-income persons through the St. Simeon's housing project. Its origins have been described in an earlier chapter. In 1995 St. Simeon's had a board dominated by members of Holy Faith, with Walter Bruce as chair and a few members from St. Bede's and the mission. A grant of $12,000 from the United Thank Offering had been used for improvements to the buildings, which were aging. In 1997 there were still questions about the relationship of St. Simeon's to Holy Faith and lawyers were asked to review the relevant documents. A report by Janet Kaye indicated that the membership of the board did not conform to the articles of incorporation, the project was falling behind financially, and there was a possibility of bankruptcy. Some changes were made and a year later Richard Simpson was able to tell the vestry that St. Simeon's was functioning much more smoothly. Holy Faith had provided $10,000 for roof repairs and all the roofs had been replaced within a three-year period. The board had been able to acquire an adjacent property and considered opening an assisted-living facility there, but in the end this was not done and the house was re-sold. As the century closed there was still concern about St. Simeon's. Some of the buildings had been refurbished and professional management had been ensured through the appointment of Nan Dieterich as overseer, but some worried about the ongoing cost of maintaining the facility and the possibility of inadequate liability insurance.

The Holy Faith library continued to play an important part in the life of the parish. In 1995 it was open every Sunday and library assistants, including Carol Sheffler, Lee Ice, and Mary Lou Stark, were available to help patrons on the first Sunday of each month. There were regular library teas followed by literary presentations and several autograph parties. In 1996 a library tea recognized twenty-four Santa Fe artists, all of them members of Holy Faith; 116 new books had been added to the collection. Warren Day, reporting for the library committee, told the vestry that the library was staffed four days a week and that a local expert had valued the holdings at $75,000. Mary Lou Stark served as librarian for a number of years. She was helped by Margaret Rymar and when illness forced her to reduce her commitment was succeeded by Virginia Horner as chair of the library committee, but she remained active in the library work. Naturally the Conkey House construction project interfered with the normal operation of the library, even though the actual library space was not altered significantly. Books had to be boxed and stored until work was complete. Their return offered an unusual opportunity for classifications to be rearranged and the catalogue placed on a computer. For a year or two the library teas were in abeyance, but they were missed and eventually reinstituted with several authors speaking on their writings.

†

As the century ended the role of the mission of Christ the King was reconsidered. We have seen that the reports studied by the long-rang planning committee emphasized the importance of planting new mission in areas of rapid population growth, and local studies had identified such areas in south Santa Fe. We have also noted the work of Fr. Ralph Bethancourt, a former assistant at Holy Faith, in founding the mission of Christ the King in the rapidly-developing suburb of El Dorado in 1993. Two years later Fr. Bethancourt renounced his Episcopal orders and was ordained a priest of the Orthodox church. He established Holy Trinity Antiochan Orthodox Church in Santa Fe and took about half of the fifty members of the mission with him. Some of the founders of the mission returned to Holy Faith. Bishop Kelshaw appointed the Rev. Michael Milligan vicar of the Episcopal mission. For a time he continued to hold services in the Seventh Day Adventist building. When this space was no longer available he moved to the El Dorado Community Center, where it was necessary to pack up the church's appointments and put them in place afresh each Sunday. Naturally members of the mission hoped for a building of their own, and this seemed to be a possibility in the year 2000 when the developers of a new subdivision, Rancho Viejo in south Santa Fe, offered them a building site near the Community College and the flourishing Catholic church Santa Maria de la Paz. Leaders of the mission said that they already had $70,000 in funding for the project in hand. The deanery had given them $10,000 and they hoped Holy Faith would contribute twice that amount. In the mean time they changed the mission's name from Christ the King, which was thought to be too male and monarchical, to the Church of the Holy Family. The vestry did not immediately take action on the mission's request for money ("Let's slow down" was Fr. Coleman's advice), but the Outreach committee did later allocate the $20,000. Building plans, however, remained in abeyance.

Following Fr. Coleman's installation as rector the previous interim priest, Fr. Ivan Weiser, remained in Santa Fe and continued to minister informally to a number of the older, more conservative members of Holy Faith. For a time they met in a private home as a "house church." The bishop then suggested that they might be organized as a chapel of ease, and eventually they were given independent status as St. Thomas' Church in Santa Fe. In 2001 thirteen communicants of Holy Faith, all members of the conservative "Forward in Faith" group, transferred to St. Thomas'. This group included such former parish leaders as Paul Brennand and Peggy Bruce.

Closer ties with St. Bede's were considered in 1998. These would have included annual pulpit exchanges for the rectors and occasional joint meetings of the two vestries. After one such exchange, however, this rapprochement did not continue, probably because the ideological positions of the parishes were too different. Under Fr. Coleman Holy Faith liked to characterize itself as traditional, "Bible-believing," and high church, while St. Bede's was more open to women priests, gay and lesbian communicants, and liturgical experimentation. Every year a few communicants moved from one of the parishes to another, evidently seeking a more congenial environment. Holy Faith did establish closer ecumenical ties with the Roman Catholic cathedral and its dean, Fr. Jerome Martínez y Alire, and with First Presbyterian church and its minister, Dr. Sheila Gustafson. It was new, unusual, and certainly desirable for the Episcopalians and their Catholic neighbors to be involved in joint activities.

During the summer of 1998 Fr. Coleman exchanged parishes with a priest from Northern England, Tony Rablen. Fr. Rablen and his family were warmly welcomed at Holy Faith. His preaching was much appreciated, even if (as he said) he had prepared sermons based on the English lectionary rather than lessons prescribed by the American Prayer Book. Bishop Michael Marshall later came to Santa Fe from London and was remembered for his healing services and for a piano recital. In adddition to Bp. Kelshaw, a number of American bishops visited the parish as well. Among these were William Frey, retired bishop of Colorado, who had trained Fr. Dinegar for the priesthood while rector at Los Alamos and returned to New Mexico in August 2000 to help celebrate the anniversary of Dinegar's diaconal ordination; John MacNaughton, retired bishop of West Texas; Maurice Benitez, retired bishop of Texas, and Roger White, bishop of Milwaukee.

✝

Fr. Coleman's annual report for 1998 described the changes he had witnessed since his arrival a year and a half earlier. He began by noting the "joyous, heavily attended parish picnic at Camp Stoney, which attracted 150 parishioners of all ages." Some were startled to see so many children. "We are bucking the downward trend that main line churches are experiencing almost everywhere we look and which we had experience here for over five years," Coleman said. "This rapid growth is almost unheard of at traditional Episcopal churches." Attendance was up 25% and pledges had doubled in two years. Nearly 30% of the church's income went to support work outside the parish. He was able to strike the same note a year later. "Fewer than three years ago," he said, "we were in decline, an aging church troubled by controversies, witnessing prospective new parishioners and young families come and go within a few weeks. We were driven by conflicting agendas and personality conflicts. No wonder we were in decline." Noel Ice, the parish treasurer, was able to report that for the first time in thirteen years none of the endowment income had been used for operating expenses in 1998, but was allocated to outreach instead. Holy Faith ranked fourth in the diocese in the number of baptized members, third in attendance, fifth in pledge and plate income, and fourth in diocesan giving and outreach. When Dr. Ice resigned as treasurer in 2000 he told the vestry that he had served "during a period of incredible growth, with a budget of $190,000 in 1995 up to over $650,000 this year." David Haskin, a relatively new parishioner who had formerly been treasurer of the diocese of Minnesota, succeeded Ice as treasurer of Holy Faith.

It remained for Richard Simpson, senior warden in the year 2000, to sum up the situation in his report to the parish. "The Church of the Holy Faith," he said, "continues its phenomenal growth. This is at a time when many Episcopal churches are, unfortunately, losing members. Our growth is not by accident. It is the result of much hard work and the efforts of our clergy and staff in their special areas and ministries." He credited Fr. Coleman with "bringing Holy Faith out of the ashes like a phoenix to where we are today." Fr. Coleman himself said that Holy Faith had moved back into the orbit of the wider Episcopal Church, partly because of the work of the new Presiding Bishop, Frank Griswold, and partly under the influence of Roger White, Bishop of Milwaukee, who made annual visits to Santa Fe for several years to speak on stewardship and relations with the national church.

All in all the Church of the Holy Faith in Santa Fe could hardly have witnessed the dawn of a new century in a more promising position.

Epilogue

Despite its reverence for history and tradition Santa Fe had changed enormously during the second half of the twentieth century. The population of the city proper had more than doubled: just under 28,000 in 1950, it had reached 60,000 by 2000. The growth of the surrounding county was even more notable, rising from a population of about 38,000 in 1950 to more than 100,000 fifty years later. Thus the total number of people in the area which might reasonably be served by the Church of the Holy Faith had risen from about 66,000 to 160,000. The proportion who were Anglo (or, as the census said, white and non-Hispanic) had increased from 34% in 1970 to 49% in 1990; the Anglo and Hispanic groups were nearly balanced as the century ended. The number of art galleries was said to have grown from 2 in 1951 to 231 in 1992, the number of architects from 9 to 89, the number of hotel rooms from 795 to 4,116.[1]

Holy Faith itself had not kept pace with this growth. In fact the number of baptized members had declined somewhat, from about 1000 in 1950 to fewer than 900 in 2000. There were several reasons for this. Holy Faith was no longer the only Episcopal church in Santa Fe: there was another parish and a mission. The proportion of the population which attended church regularly had declined from a high immediately following World War II. The membership of main-line denominations like the Episcopal, Presbyterian, and Methodist churches had fallen as a proportion of the total population. More and more persons had been

---

[1] Figures from Chris Wilson, *The Myth Of Santa Fe* (Albuquerque, 1997), pp. 330-31. For further comments about changes in Santa Fe see Henry J. Tobias and Charles E. Woodhouse, *Santa Fe: A Modern History, 1880-1990* (Albuquerque, 2001), esp. pp. 193-235.

drawn into new churches, often holding fundamentalist or charismatic beliefs. Santa Fe in particular had become home to a number of "new age" religious groups, some claiming to be Christian and others, like the Wiccans and the Sikhs, clearly outside that faith.

It is unfortunate that no demographic survey of the Holy Faith congregation was made at the end of the century, so any comments about its composition must be impressionistic rather than based on hard figures. It is clear, however, that the parish, like the city which it served, was unusual. Since Santa Fe attracted so many retired persons who had left careers in other places, it was natural that a number of them would come to Holy Faith. Those who had become parishioners included doctors, lawyers, professors, and business executives who had formerly lived in such places as Dallas, Ft. Worth, Austin, El Paso, Kansas City, and Minneapolis. A number had special skills and experiences in church-related activities: some had been members of vestries or cathedral chapters, wardens, parish or diocesan treasurers, church musicians, members of the board of seminaries and other church-related institutions, or creators of liturgical art. Since they were retired, they often had time available to give to the church. In some cases their skills were put to work eagerly, while in others there seemed to be little place for them. The parish naturally included also those who had been members for many years and were still active, together–fortunately–with a number of younger members who had children at home. In earlier years it had been said that the church was not welcoming to newcomers, but efforts had been made to change this situation and visitors and those who had moved to the area were generally given a friendly reception.

The parishioners were not diverse in ethnic make-up. Virtually all were (to use Santa Fe terminology) Anglos, with no blacks or Asians and only a few of Hispanic descent. Some were wealthy and virtually all enjoyed comfortable economic conditions. A majority held conservative views in both politics and churchmanship. In this they followed the lead of the diocese and the parish, both of which were considerably more traditional in outlook that the average parish in the American Episcopal Church. Although the leaders of both diocese and parish talked more favorably of the national establishment than they had done a decade earlier, at the end of the twentieth century they had not yet restored the full payment of funds requested by the national church. Some new members had come to the Episcopal church from other denominations and had little experience of what it was like to be part of a national and international Anglican communion rather than an independent local gathered fellowship. Naturally some of those who had transferred to Holy Faith from other Episcopal churches were disappointed not to have closer ties to the larger Episcopal community. Some also missed the variety of liturgies they had experienced elsewhere, including Rite II services, frequent Evensongs, and the occasional use of sung Morning Prayer. The older group of those who hankered for the services of the 1928 Prayer Book appeared to be gradually disappearing.

If this analysis is correct, what does it suggest for the future of the church? While no one can safely predict the future, the prospects appeared to be good. The parish was growing. It included a number of members with a special concern for the church and resources, both of time and money, to support its work. Throughout its history Holy Faith had experienced divisions of opinion among members and it was inevitable that it would continue to do so, but most parishioners were endowed with a spirit of charity and tolerance and were willing to live with those whose views were somewhat different from their own. It seemed unlikely that the parish would ever again be dominated by powerful anti-clerical lay leaders who tried to dictate policies for years at a time. This was a tradition that can be traced back to the days of Bradford Prince, and it was a notable feature of the 1980s.[2] It was not likely that the church would ever again enjoy the close relationship to civic political leadership that had characterized its early years. It was inevitable that the coming years would bring cyclical ups and downs rather than a continually rising curve. This was in keeping with the church's past history and a common aspect of Episcopal parishes throughout the country. Even Phoenixes do not rise continually. But both past history and present circumstances suggested that the Church of the Holy Faith would remain a strong presence in the city of Santa Fe and in the Diocese of the Rio Grande.

---

[2] The rector of St. Bede's, the Rev. Richard Murphy, liked to refer to these leaders as "lay popes" and said that there were enough of them to make up a Vatican Council in Santa Fe.

Appendix 1
CHURCH OF THE HOLY FAITH, STATISTICS, 1953-2000

Year	Baptized Members	Communicants	Church School Students	Total Attendance
1953	1027	722	208	21,045
1954	1068	682	250	21,995
1955	1112	716	285	22,563
1956	1145	763	288	26,309
1957	1170	783	301	23,105
1958	1232	805	320	25,347
1959	1253	824	342	27,145
1960	1302	857	291	25,896
1961	1371	882	312	26,381
1962	1096	692	203	26,809
1963	1115	710	210	22,688
1964	1034	709	196	21,179
1965	804	524	128	19,035
1966	868	571	121	14,629
1967	749	550	99	17,253
1968	594	553	86	15,752
1969	739	555	86	16,524
1970	771	577	88	16,321
1971	804	605	56	12,669
1972	808	629	138*	17,085
1973	790	660	147*	19,523
1974	827	622	115*	19,585
1975	869	627	—	18,741
1976	902	635	100*	20,070
1977	938	654	87*	19,549
1978	974	677	66*	18,937
1979	760	651	69*	20,123
1980	800	676	95*	20,057
1981	825	684	106*	21,737
1982	860	684	39	22,208
1983	898	684	98	21,627

1984	786	662	80	22,332
1985**	786	662	49	19,174
1986	823	749	55	20,935
1987	857	789	58	20,652
1988	898	816	58	20,323
1989	935	850	50	24,150
1990	818	670	50	26,635
1991	881	716	47	21,166
1992	909	736	62	20,510
1993	905	718	32	18,062
1994	733	556	38	16,389
1995	752	572	21	14,216
1996	745	568	24	18,385
1997	744	570	51	22,091
1998	780	595	67	23,268
1999	833	623	81	25,744
2000	870	647	142	28,129

---

* Includes adults.

** Incomplete data; the same figures were used for two years.

Total attendance figures for 1996 and 1998-2000 are estimates based on average weekly attendance plus attendance at Christmas, Easter, and at weekday services. Actual total attendance figures are not available for those years.

Appendix 2
CHURCH OF THE HOLY FAITH, STAFF

I. Rectors

Leonidas W. Smith, 1912-18

Walter S. Trowbridge, 1918-35

Charles J. Kinsolving III, 1936-53

Henry F. Seaman, 1954-65

Richard H. Williams, 1965-67

Dennis Walker, 1967-72

Donald L. Campbell, 1972-85

Jaquelin Washington, interim, 1985-86

Jon Simms Receconi, 1986-87

Philip Wainwright, 1988-94

Ivan Weiser, interim, 1994-96

Dale Coleman, 1996-

II. Curates, Assistants, or Associate Rectors

Bernard Lee Short, Jr., 1958-60

William E. Crews, 1961-62

Alfred C. Krader, 1964-65

Dennis Walker, 1966-67

Harold Edmonson, 1968

Elvin R. Gallagher, 1968-71

W. James Marner, 1973-77

Michael O'Connell, 1979-80

James Adams, 1980-82

Kenneth Shepard, 1982-85

Philip Wainwright, 1986-88

Pascal Nelson, 1988-91

Ralph Bethancourt, 1991-93

Logan Craft, 1999-2002

Jon Anderson, 2002-

III. Organists, Choir Directors, and Directors of Music

Joseph F. Leonard, 1956-58

Jerrell J. Surface, 1959

Mark Davis, 1960-66
Mary Jean Cook, 1966-72
Harriet Heltman, 1972
W. James Marner, 1973-77
Daniel G. Kelley, choir director, 1978-83
Mrs. Daniel Kelley, organist, 1978-79
Gregory Wilcoxson, organist, 1979-82
Rebecca Rollett, 1983-95
Anthony Rollett, assistant, 1990-95
Richard Stark, 1995-97
Dianne Brehmer Bailey, organist, 1997-98
David Arellanes, choir director, 1997-2000
Michael Case, organist, 1998-
Gerald Near, director of music, 2000-

BISHOPS
Bishops of the Missionary District
   Frederick B. Howden, 1914-1940
   Frederick B. Bartlett, 1940-1941
   James M. Stoney, 1942-1952
Bishops of the Diocese
   James M. Stoney, 1952-1956
   Charles J. Kinsolving III, 1956-1972
   Richard M. Trelease, Jr., 1972-1987
   William Davidson, interim, 1987-1988
   Terence Kelshaw, 1988-

APPENDIX

Appendix 3
HOLY FAITH ANNUAL BUDGETS, 1985-2000

Year	Budgeted Income	Pledges	Rector's Salary	Curate's Salary	To Diocese	Special Ministries
1986	162,300	137,000	26,000	—	45,658	31,625
1987	196,440	193,500	26,400	17,700	19,961 [sic]	59,075
1988	236,145	203,310	25,225	8,100	51,435	39,631
		(includes plate)		(6 months)		
1989	307,400	167,400	26,400	18,150	65,400	27,007
1990	314,600	185,000	27,600	20,000	51,900	30,800
1991	322,842	200,000	28,800	20,900	56,700	32,300
1992	304,920*	230,000	28,800	21,000	67,082	26,082
1993	315,000	250,000	31,800	24,000	69,300	29,300
1994	330,560	205,000	32,754	—	58,630	25,100
1995	337,650	150,000	25,930	—	59,750	20,510
1996	375,000	206,500	85,000#	—	50,600	37,000
1997	422,604	270,000	73,325#	—	50,800	43,120
1998	667,692	375,000	79,308#	—	64,520	43,190
1999	807,169	422,840	133,114#	—	72,578	67,340
2000	839,753	522,846	151,419#	—	75,684	73,847

* From 1992 on these figures do not include endowment interest allocated to Special Ministries, as earlier budgets do.
# Includes all clergy expenses.

Appendix 4
YEAR-END VALUE OF ENDOWMENT, 1985-2000*

1985	$1,313,141
1986	1,092,280
1987	1,191,400
1988	1,611,545
1989	1,125,724
1990	1,126,350
1991	1,664,948
1992	1,529,037
1993	2,020,705
1994	2,167,085
1995	2,798,342
1996	2,353,995
1997	2,697,396
1998	3,172,420
1999	3,395,192
2000	3,244,704

---

* More accurately this is the total value of invested funds, some of which were designated as capital reserves rather than endowment. In 1996 the annual meeting adopted a resolution stating that the endowment itself was $1,200,000; this then had a market value of $1,349,895.

Index

INDEX

216

ALSO FROM LPD PRESS

LPD PRESS
925 SALAMANCA NW
ALBUQUERQUE, NEW MEXICO 87107-5647
505/344-9382 FAX 505/345-5129
INFO@NMSANTOS.COM WWW.NMSANTOS.COM